Leader's Guide for

Discipleship

by J. Heinrich Arnold

The Plough Publishing House

Farmington, PA 15437, USA
Robertsbridge, East Sussex TN32 5DR, U.K.

Cover art: Vincent van Gogh. *The Sower.* Arles, 1888
© E.G. Bührle Foundation, Zurich. Used with permission.

Discipleship Leader's Guide ISBN:0-87486-089-X

First Printing	Feb. 1997
Second Printing	March 1997
Third Printing	July 1997

Library of Congress Cataloging-in-Publication Data for Original Title

Arnold, J. Heinrich. 1913–
　　Discipleship / compiled and edited by the Bruderhof communities:
　foreword by Henri J. M. Nouwen.
　　　p.　cm.
　　ISBN 0-87486-066-0
　　1. Bruderhof communities—Doctrines.　2. Christian life—
　Bruderhof community authors.　3. Arnold, J. Heinrich, 1913–　.
　4. Christian communities—United States.　I. Bruderhof
　communities (Rifton, N.Y.)
　II. Title.
　BX8129.65.A76　1994
　289.7'3—dc20　　　　　　　　　　　　　94–33910
　　　　　　　　　　　　　　　　　　　　　　　CIP

Printed in USA

Contents

Why a Leader's Guide?

Heinrich Arnold's book, *Discipleship*, is best read with others. It is a book to be shared. As Henri Nouwen writes in his Foreword, "Arnold's words come from his deep experience in community, where discipleship is lived. It is in community that we are tested and purified." Discipleship is not a solitary journey. We need each other as we seek to be faithful disciples of Jesus. Though following Jesus begins with a decision that only an individual can make, that decision is not a private affair. If Jesus called together a family of disciples, following him must mean taking a shared path.

The purpose of this *Leader's Guide* is to help foster a discipleship that is lived out with others. It is designed to aid the leader in helping his or her group grow together. Its aim is not only to stimulate open discussion, or to determine the meaning and relevance of particular passages, but also to encourage a deeper sense of community.

Using this Guide

This Guide is intended as a supplement to *Discipleship,* not as a substitute for it.

Because of its format, you do not need to read *Discipleship* in its entirety before leading a study of it. In fact, it is not a book to be read in one sitting, or even in a week or two. It is to be read "existentially;" that is, meditatively, reflectively, and inwardly. The *Leader's Guide* is geared toward this end. The aim is not discussion itself, but the shared discovery of how Arnold's words can be applied to everyday life.

Although *Discipleship* can be read and discussed in a variety of settings and time-frames, it lends itself best to groups that will be together over a longer period of time. Following Jesus is itself a lifetime journey, and this book reflects that. Though most of the passages are short, the thoughts contained in them are deep and often profound. This is a book to be pondered, not just read. And the more the group can share life together, the more alive the book will become.

The *Leader's Guide* is not so much a blueprint, as a map, and should be used in conjunction with the leader's creativity and the group's involvement. Participants must come prepared, already conversant with each chapter's content. So must the leader. But the leader must also be sensitive and take into account the particularities of his or her group and context. Various settings and needs will determine various ways of using the guide. Be flexible. Not all the material can or should be used. Some questions will lead to more fruitful exchanges than others.

Format

This Guide consists of 24 Sessions. Because the chapters are relatively short, they lend themselves to a weekly study. However, depending on the size of your group and the length of time you have together, several sessions can be combined into a single study.

Each session consists of four basic sections. You may want to emphasize one section over the others. However, the sections do relate to and reinforce each other.

Starting Together This part contains a question or activity which will help the group engage the chapter and each other. Be aware that while it is easy to share from one's head only, it is also a temptation to honor emotions that disregard questions of truth and meaning. The aim of this section is to draw the group into the book and toward each other. This will help to create a secure space to share openly and honestly.

Studying Together Good questions can produce fruitful responses. A good discussion rarely happens by accident. The right question is often the key to stimulating worthwhile sharing. To help facilitate this, three groups of questions can be asked: (1) *Focus Questions* help the group to get into the book itself. What is Arnold saying? What points is he trying to make? What are the main themes of the chapter? (2) *Discovery Questions* go deeper and deal with the meaning or implications of Arnold's words. What relevance does this chapter have? (3) *Impact Questions* focus on how this chapter makes a difference in one's life and in the life of the group. They are more direct, calling for change and challenging the group toward deeper commitment and accountability. (4) *Leader's Questions* provides space for the group leader to write down discussion questions of his or her own.

Stretching Each Other Every group and each person can be stretched to go beyond where they are. If discipleship is a journey, it is a journey of transformation. Most of us, however, resist being changed. For this very reason we need the challenge of being stretched. Each study therefore includes an activity or exercise to help make the chapter more "alive."

Going Forward How you end your time together is important. Singing, praying, or being quiet together are all appropriate ways to close a session. Emphasize that each participant should continue to "study" until the next session and seek to personally apply what he or she has learned during the current session.

If participants wish to continue sharing after a session, this should be encouraged. But there needs to be a closing time to free those who need to meet other commitments.

Corresponding Study Guide

To complement the *Leader's Guide*, there is a *Study Guide* that individuals in your group can use during the week. A book study involves preparation, both on the group's part as well as the leader's. Participants need time beforehand to reflect on what they read. Encourage the group to come prepared. At the very least, ask them to read the chapter in question beforehand. Though the *Study Guide* is optional and should be used only if it is a help, it does provide thought-provoking questions which challenge the reader to go deeper than they might otherwise go.

Emphasize that each chapter in the book should be read *before* going on to answering the questions in the *Study Guide*. Also point out that the *Study Guide* is not a homework assignment. Filling it out mechanically accomplishes nothing. The point of each study is to stimulate the reader to consider Arnold's words in ways that they might not have thought of by themselves. Hopefully it will encourage the group to come with questions of their own.

Helps and Hints for Leaders

- Before you lead, personally apply! Do not lead if you are not willing to follow. Make sure the questions you ask of the group are also questions you have asked yourself.

- Plan ahead. Decide when each session will begin, where it will be held, how long it will be, and how many weeks it will last. Begin and end promptly. Always come prepared.

- Before you begin your study, discuss as a group why it is important that no one dominate and why each person's contribution is important.

- Encourage quiet members to share. Ask them, by name, "Do you have anything to add?" Remind the group that there are rarely ever right or wrong answers. Usually, every thought has merit. All questions are valid. And some questions may have several answers.

- Ask for volunteers to read different chapter selections or scripture verses that are highlighted. Group participation is key!

- Whenever you can, link various responses. Feel free to adjust the order of your questions in light of where the discussion is moving. In short, help the group see the connections and, whenever you can, reinforce what gets brought out.

- Don't be afraid to bring the group back to the question or subject at hand if they stray too far for too long. Keep the discussion moving and focused.

- Do not feel compelled to cover all the material. Adapt each study for your particular purposes and needs.

- Be prepared to rephrase the question. Some questions are difficult and may not elicit an immediate response. Don't be afraid of a silent pause. If no response is forthcoming, begin the discussion by offering your insights. Then invite further comments.

- Participate, but don't dominate! Insights that come from the group are much more meaningful and transforming than those taught by the leader.

- Never impose an agenda. Remind participants that the questions you ask are meant to generate, not dictate, discussion. Be open to how God's Spirit leads.

- To give the discussion greater depth, ask questions like, "Why?" or "Why do you believe that?" "Why is this important?" "Does anyone feel differently?"

- You may want to limit the size of your group so as to facilitate better discussion. If your group is large, break it down into smaller groups for more in-depth sharing.

- *Discipleship* is sprinkled throughout with scripture references. Arnold's thoughts often grow directly out of a biblical passage. Refer your group to these passages often.

- Be ready for unexpected twists and turns, but always remind the group that the aim of the study is to discover how to follow Jesus more faithfully. Talking is not enough.

Foreword & Introduction

Preparing

Decide beforehand whether or not to give a copy of *Discipleship*, along with a copy of the *Study Guide*, to your group before you meet the first time. Before your first meeting, skim the contents of *Discipleship* to get an overview. Look at the topics it covers. Familiarize yourself with Arnold's style. Read the Foreword and Introduction. These will form the basis of your first meeting.

In addition to the book, familiarize yourself with this *Leader's Guide*. Read the Introduction and note how each section is structured and the kinds of questions that will be asked. Also become familiar with the *Study Guide* if your group will be using it. Note that it contains many of the same questions as the *Leader's Guide*.

Make sure you have enough copies of *Discipleship* and the *Study Guide* to distribute at your first meeting if you haven't already done so. Also, determine beforehand how much time you want to devote for informal gathering, refreshments, singing, or anything else that might happen during your first meeting together.

This may be the first time your group has met together. If it is, make sure the atmosphere will encourage dialogue and sharing. Arrange your seating so that people can see one another.

For further recommended reading: *The Cost of Discipleship*, by Dietrich Bonhoeffer.

Getting Started

- Depending on the nature of your group, it will be important that people have time to get to know each other. If your group is new, have them pair off with someone they do not know. After a few minutes, gather again and have different ones introduce each other. Consider other activities that will facilitate getting to know one another.

- Take time to have the participants share why they are interested is studying *Discipleship* together. Explain to them your role as a leader and your hopes for group participation. Ask them what they feel the key ingredients for open sharing are. Be sure to emphasize the following: *respect, the ability to listen, and humility (openness to being corrected)*.

- Now pass around some copies of the illustration entitled: "Who Are You?" (Appendix B). Have the group share which child best describes the state of their faith – where they are at spiritually – and why. After a time of sharing, help the group see that being a disciple, a follower of Jesus, is not an automatic journey. We are all at different places, spiritually speaking, and we need each other's help. Faithful discipleship is a shared venture. It is not for lone rangers.

Studying Together

Reemphasize that this is a *group* study. From the Introduction, explain who Heinrich Arnold is and the kind of church community he pastored. (See Appendix A: *About the Bruderhof*) Then read the Foreword by Henri Nouwen aloud, unless the group has already had a chance to read it for themselves.

Focus Questions

1. What are some of the adjectives or images Nouwen uses to describe *Discipleship*?

2. Nouwen shares how in first reading *Discipleship* he discovered resistance in himself. Why? Has this ever happened to you while reading a book? When?

3. What, according to Nouwen, makes Arnold's words so healing? From the Introduction, are there any words Arnold expresses that exemplify this?

Discovery Questions

1. Is it possible for people to speak, as Nouwen says of Arnold, "unpopular but truly healing words" (p. x)? Can you cite examples from your own life when this has happened? Did Jesus ever do this? When?

2. How, exactly, does the Gospel ask for a "radical choice, a choice that is not always praised, supported, and celebrated" (p. ix)? How is this true in today's culture? How has this been true in your own life?

3. Nouwen emphasizes that it is in community that discipleship is lived. This was certainly true in Arnold's life. Why do you think he says this? Why might community and discipleship belong together?

4. How would you define discipleship or being a disciple? At the beginning of the book, Arnold is quoted as saying: "Discipleship is not a question of our doing; it is a matter of making room for God so that he can live in us." What point do you think Arnold is trying to make?

5. The editors write how Arnold "could not tolerate indifference to the demands of the Gospel" (p. xv). What do you think he means by this? Where might you see such tolerance today? How might you be guilty of it?

Impact Questions

1. On a spectrum between independence (being a lone ranger) and dependence (having to always be around others), where might your walk with Christ lie? How much of your life is a *shared life* with others? Where might you be guilty of a lone ranger Christianity?

2. How can the group move in the direction of community? What kinds of things need to happen if meeting together once a week (or month) is not enough? Is a greater sense of community something the group wants?

3. What would making more room for God involve for your life *right now*? Is your heart the kind of place God can live? What kind of heart would that be?

4. As a group, are we ready and willing to dare and speak to each other an unpopular but truly healing word? Can we make such a commitment with each other? How might the following verse help us in this? (See Eph. 4:15–16.)

5. Arnold writes: "We are tired of words; they are cheap and can be heard almost anywhere" (p. xv). Where in your life has your talk been greater than your walk?

Leader's Questions

_____

_____

_____

_____

_____

_____

_____

_____

_____

_____

_____

Stretching Each Other

Who in your life have you been avoiding in terms of speaking an unpopular but truly healing word? Will you dare to do so? Without gossiping about this other person, ask someone in the group to hold you accountable to do this.

Going Forward

Nouwen writes that, "This is truly a Christ-centered book." Either in song, prayer, or scripture reading, close your time together by focusing on Christ, the one we are to follow.

Notes & Announcements

_____

_____

_____

_____

_____

_____

_____

_____

The Inner Life

Preparing

As you read this chapter (pp. 1–10), notice the two main themes that emerge. It opens up with words about the significance of one's inner life (pp. 1–4), and then moves on to the importance of prayer (pp. 4–10). The connection between these two is crucial. As you prepare for this week's session, ask God to speak to your heart. Listen and seek his will, both for yourself and for the group. You will want to highlight the connection between inner vitality and prayer throughout this session.

For further recommended reading: *Inner Land*, by Eberhard Arnold (Plough Publishing House).

Getting Started

Pass around a copy of the illustration entitled: "Roots & Fruits" (Appendix C). Discuss the differences between the three trees. The picture is meant to be a visual aid to illustrate the relationship between our inner life (our roots) and outer life (fruit). Discuss all the ways we can compare our spiritual life with that of a growing tree. (*E.g., deep roots in God are necessary to weather the elements of the world.*)

This activity is meant to illustrate what Arnold says about the complete change Christ wants to bring about in our lives – from the inside out. Notice some of the principles that emerge from this illustration:

- It is a complete change that Jesus wants to bring about in our lives. Discipleship is all about a journey of total transformation, from within to without.

- The inner and the outer dimensions of our lives belong together. True change includes both.

- The deeper, more far reaching change that occurs inwardly results in a greater, more radical change outwardly.

Studying Together

Focus Questions

1. What are some of the key topics or ideas that Arnold addresses in this chapter? Do you see any connection between them?

2. From what you have read thus far, in Arnold's view, how powerful can Christ be in a person's life?

3. How would you describe Arnold's understanding of prayer? How important is it? What can it accomplish? What are we to pray for? What does Christ want most from us? (See p. 5.)

Discovery Questions

1. What passage from this chapter struck your heart most? How do you hope to be changed because of it?

2. Do you agree that people today are only "vaguely aware that there is something wrong with their inner [spiritual] life" (p. 1)? What indications are there that this is true?

3. Arnold says that once our inner person really changes, everything else, including the practical and economic areas of our lives, will change. Can you think of some examples from Scripture of how this is true? How has this been true in your life, or anyone you may personally know?

    - *Biblical figures you could cite as examples of this kind of radical change are Moses, David, Peter, and Paul.*

    - *Further examples of how God can bring about a radical change can be seen in what occurred in the early church as recorded in Acts. Arnold cites Acts 2: 37ff (p. 1). Another good example is what happened in Ephesus. (See Acts 19.)*

4. If we are destined to "judge the angels" and become "temples for God," (pp. 2–3) what kind of inner change must take place in our lives?

5. According to Arnold, can we *really* change ourselves? How is true change brought about? What is the key to real transformation?

6. Arnold asserts: "If you try to fight your emotions with other emotions, you will only become more confused" (p. 6). Have you ever experienced this? How so?

7. Arnold quotes Eph. 3:16–19. Read it together. He says: "If we were to grasp this one passage, we would understand the whole Gospel" (p. 4). How is this passage of scripture filled with good news?

8. Arnold warns against "stupidity." What does he mean by this? When are we in danger of harming our conscience, or not listening to God?

9. Arnold writes: "We should always believe that our prayers will be answered, even if they are not answered straight away" (p. 9). Has this ever been true in your life? Can you think of any passage in scripture that affirms this?

10. Arnold claims that "Long prayers are not always effective. Jesus even warns us against them. They are usually more pagan than Christian" (p. 7). What teaching of Jesus do you think Arnold is referring to? (See Mt. 6:7.) Is Arnold arguing that long prayers are necessarily wrong? Why might long prayers be pagan? What, exactly, is wrong with them?

Impact Questions

1. When you pray, what kinds of things do you usually pray for? How might you be guilty of making "selfish requests" in Jesus' name (p. 9.)?

2. Are you finding a quiet space every day to pray? If not, why? Is it difficult for you to become inwardly quiet? Why? What does Arnold mean by this? Why is quietness so important?

3. Is prayer as important to you as water? What place could you set aside as your "closet" to pray? Where will that be?

4. What would it take for you to gain "a heart that listens to God alone" (p. 5)? What voices in your life crowd out the voice of God? *Have the group contrast the voice of God with the voice of others. When God speaks, what happens? When other voices vie for attention, what happens? Compare and contrast these two voices, where they lead and what results. You may want to use a blackboard.*

When God Speaks	Competing Voices

Leader's Questions

_____

_____

_____

_____

_____

_____

_____

_____

_____

_____

Stretching Each Other

What in your life are you overly attached to? *(An attachment is anything other than God that drives you, defines who you are, or gives you a sense of significance or security. An attachment is something you would find terribly difficult to live without. To let go of it would make you feel naked.)* How might this be an obstacle to hearing God's voice in your life? Take time to have the group share what this might be.

Going Forward

Arnold writes: "If we hear nothing from God for a long time, it may be because there is something between us and heaven" (p. 4). To end your time together, have the group spend some time in silence asking God to reveal anything that might be between them and heaven. Emphasize the importance of listening to one's conscience.

Remind them of what Arnold says on p. 5: "We must give him our innermost being, our heart and soul. When we give ourselves completely over to him – when we no longer resist giving him our whole person and whole personality – then he can help us first by bringing us to bankruptcy and then by filling us with true life."

Notes & Announcements

_____

_____

_____

_____

_____

_____

_____

Repentance & Conversion

Preparing

Before you read these two chapters (pp. 11–20), write down what "repentance" means to you. Is it a positive, or negative thing? What feelings come to you as you reflect on repentance? Can you determine why you feel as you do?

Repentance is a much misunderstood word. As you read this chapter note what Arnold says repentance is and what it is not. To help you grasp the importance and meaning of repentance, reflect on the following scripture passages:

- Mt. 3:1–12 — Lk. 3:1–18
- Lk. 24:40–49
- Acts 2:37–41
- Rom. 2:4—2 Pet. 3:9

After reading these passages, how would you describe repentance? Is it a matter of God's judgment alone? Is repentance a punishment or a gift? How radical or significant is repentance? What results from a repentant heart?

For further recommended reading: *The Pursuit of God,* by A.W. Tozer.

Getting Started

Pass around of piece a paper and make sure each person in the group has a pen or pencil to write with. Number it from 1 to 15. Read the following little scenario and ask the group the questions below. Have

them choose between one of three alternatives: (T) True; (F) False;
(?) Can't Determine.

*A businessman had just turned off the lights in the store when a man ap-
peared and demanded money. The owner opened a cash register. The contents of the cash register were scooped up and the man sped away. A member
of the police force was notified promptly.*

1. A man appeared after the owner had turned off his store
   lights .... T F ?

2. The robber was a man .... T F ?

3. The man who appeared did not demand money .... T F ?

4. The man who opened the cash register was the owner .. T F ?

5. The store owner scooped up the contents of the cash
   register and ran away .... T F ?

6. Someone opened a cash register .... T F ?

7. After the man, who demanded the money, scooped up
   the contents of the cash register, he ran away .... T F ?

8. While the cash register contained money, the story does not
   state how much .... T F ?

9. The robber demanded money of the owner .... T F ?

10. The robber opened the cash register .... T F ?

11. After the store lights were turned off a man appeared ... T F ?

12. The robber did not take the money with him .... T F ?

13. The robber did not demand money of the owner .... T F ?

14. The owner opened a cash register .... T F ?

15. Taking the contents of the cash register with him, the
    man ran out of the store .... T F ?

Most in your group will assume that this is a story about a robbery. But it isn't! It is a story about a security guard who comes to collect and deliver to the bank a store owner's earnings. The police is promptly notified that the collection was made.

This exercise is meant to illustrate how everything changes when one's framework changes. It provides an analogy of what happens when one experiences repentance and conversion: everything is turned upside-down. Life is radically altered. Use this exercise as a lead-in to the subject of repentance and conversion.

Studying Together

Focus Questions

1. Arnold says, "The Gospel begins with a call to repentance" (p. 11). How does Arnold understand repentance? What does repentance not mean? *(Have the group contrast these.)*

What Repentance Means	What Repentance does not Mean

2. How is repentance brought about? How does a person really change? Is self-determination enough?

3. What must we do for our part to repent?

4. How is conversion different from repentance? How might the metaphor "rebirth" help us understand its meaning?

5. In experiencing conversion, what is the most important thing?

Discovery Questions

1. Read some of the scriptures below. How do they help you better understand repentance?

   • Mt. 3: 1–12 — Lk. 3:1–18

   • Lk. 24:40–49

   • Acts 2:37–41

   • Rom. 2:4 — 2 Pet. 3:9

2. Is repentance simply turning away from sin, or is it something more? What does the Kingdom of God have to do with repentance? (Note how Arnold refers to becoming "fit for God's new future" on p. 14. Explain how this makes repentance something positive and affirming.)

3. For Arnold, why is repentance a gift? What quality of God does the call to repentance come from?

4. Who or what kind of people find it most difficult to repent? Why is this? How might Luke 18:9–14 provide an answer to this question?

5. Arnold says, we must "drop everything, including everything we count as positive in ourselves" (p. 18). Why is this? What is he referring to?

6. How radical a change is there when a sinner repents? How does 2 Cor. 5:17 answer this? Can a repentant life be seen by others?

7. Is repentance a matter of attitude alone? Why not? Is it a matter of simply getting one's act together or changing one's behavior?

8. Arnold claims that "Half-hearted Christianity is worse than no Christianity" (p. 19). Why is this? How might Rev. 3: 14–16 speak to this?

9. What is the key to bearing good fruit? Why is a *personal relationship* with Jesus (instead of the moral law or a worthy ideal) essential?

Impact Questions

1. In what way might you be guilty of being too religious? Where might there be a scribe or Pharisee in you? In what ways do we try to project a "good" self-image?

2. Arnold says: "Many Christians are attracted by his promise of salvation, but they do not want to repent fully" (p. 11). How might this be true in your life?

3. Arnold warns that "we must not play with God's goodness" (p. 13). What do you think he means by this and where might you be guilty of doing this? Are you determined to stop playing with his goodness? What will need to become different in your life?

4. Arnold writes: "At first, the closer you come to God the more you will feel judged by your sin, but in the end you will find deep joy and peace" (p. 14). Recall how this has been true in your life. Is there anything hindering you from experiencing this again?

5. Have you been "personally confronted by Jesus himself?" Does he really rule your life?

Leader's Questions

_____

_____

_____

_____

_____

_____

_____

_____

_____

_____

Stretching Each Other

Arnold writes: "If we are to bear good fruit, we must repent and be purified again and again." In other words, repentance isn't a one time thing. Conversion is an ongoing process. John the Baptist spoke of producing fruit in keeping with repentance. When the crowd heard him, they asked John what to do and he gave some pretty specific answers. Where might you need to specifically repent? In what way(s) might the group need to repent? Can you share specifically, pointing first to yourself?

Going Forward

To close your time together read from Arnold's letter on page 16. Spend time in silence. Have each person ask Christ to unmuddy the cloudy water in his or her own heart. Ask the Holy Spirit to turn your eyes toward God, toward his love and forgiveness.

Notes & Announcements

_____

_____

_____

_____

_____

_____

_____

_____

Faith & Dogmatism

Preparing

These two chapters (pp. 21–33), like the previous two, belong together. Reflect for a moment, before you read, why this is so. How is a living faith different from simply assenting to the truth of certain doctrines or principles? How would you contrast a true believer and a "dogmatist?" Who might the dogmatists have been in Jesus' time? Who might they be today?

For further recommended reading: *Living Faith*, by Jacques Ellul.

Getting Started

Have the group read about Abraham in Hebrews 11: 8–12,17–19. Imagine that instead of being a man of faith, Abraham had been a dogmatist. How might things have been different? What kinds of things would a dogmatist think or say if he were in Abraham's situation?

Studying Together

As you look at these two chapters, remember that Arnold is not trying to cover everything that could be said on these two subjects. In fact, it is enlightening to think about what Arnold does not say. For example, he does not try to define faith as such. Nor does he dwell long on the relationship between faith and reason. His approach to faith is a more simple, yet profound one. As you discuss the questions below, keep the discussion focused and away from too much speculation.

Focus Questions

1. According to Arnold, what is the key to finding God?

2. From these two chapters, how would you describe faith? Find as many adjectives as you can to describe faith. Is faith a work of God only? Is it merely a matter of "receiving."

3. How is faith to be guarded? What hinders faith from growing?

4. How is a true believer different from a dogmatist? How would you describe a dogmatist or a dogmatic spirit?

Discovery Questions

1. Why is *faith*, in particular, the one essential thing for finding God? *(Note: For any relationship to grow, faith must be at the center. Genuine knowledge of another is impossible without faith and trust.)*

2. Arnold writes: "Faith and a good conscience are completely interwoven with one another" (p. 22). Why is this? Read Titus 1:15–16 and Romans 14 and discuss how faith and a good conscience belong together.

3. How does Arnold see the relationship between faith and understanding? Is intellectual proof of any real help to faith? Why not? Does this mean faith is irrational? What is the surest means for understanding?

4. Why do so many people today find it difficult to have faith? (See pp. 25–26.) Can you think of other reasons why people have a hard time believing?

5. Why is dogmatism an enemy of faith? How can a "right principle" become deadly? Have you ever experienced this to be true in your own life? Who in Jesus' day were dogmatists? Who might they be today?

6. Arnold says: "We must become 'narrow' in the right way" (p. 30). What does he mean? Can one be narrow and still have a broad heart? How so?

7. Are "forms" or traditions the real enemy of faith, or is there something else at issue? Why is a formless Christianity anti-Christian? *(Note the relevance of the Incarnation. God took on human flesh. True spirituality is earthly.)*

Impact Questions

1. Arnold says that "To question God's love and his nearness leads to death for someone who has already given him his life" (p. 26). Is there any area in your life where you are especially doubting God's great mercy? Can you share this?

2. Jesus warns against worry (Lk. 12:22–26). Where in your life do you worry too much?

3. Have you ever become (or are you now) obsessed by a principle, however right or true? What principles might your group have that are overly dogmatic?

4. Arnold warns against separating faith from experience (p. 30). How might your profession of faith go beyond what you actually live or experience?

Leader's Questions

_____

_____

_____

_____

_____

_____

_____

_____

_____

_____

Stretching Each Other

It is easy to see the dogmatic spirit in others but not in oneself. As people share their struggle in this area, put out a challenge to have the group give feedback. As this is done, make sure they do this in love. We are all guilty of dogmatism, of being "too principled." This exercise is not a matter of pointing the finger. Rather, it's a matter of helping each other in ways we might be blind. If it would be more helpful, have the group break down into twos or threes.

Going Forward

To close your time, challenge the group to consider speaking to or writing a letter to someone they have hurt because of being overly dogmatic. This should be a letter of confession and asking for forgiveness. Then spend time in corporate confession, asking God to forgive any lack of faith or lovelessness.

Notes & Announcements

Commitment & Trust

Preparing

Before you read these two chapters (pp. 34–37; 68–72) think about the needs of your group. How do you feel it is going? Are you getting good participation from everybody? Are people opening themselves up?

Like repentance and conversion, commitment and trust belong together. Think about the ways they reinforce each other. Can you have one without the other? Why not?

For further recommended reading: *From Brokenness to Community,* by Jean Vanier.

Getting Started

Using a large medium to write on, have the group describe what commitment looks like – whether that commitment is to a cause, or to a person, or to a project. How do you know when a person is really committed to something or to someone? After you get a good list together, discuss the role trust plays in commitment. Can you have one without the other? Why is trust important?

Studying Together

Focus Questions

1. What is Arnold's understanding of commitment? What is a dedicated person like? What is the opposite of commitment?

2. Describe the person who trusts in Christ. Where does faith reside? What might the opposite of faith be?

3. What is the final answer to life's perplexities and problems?

Discovery Questions

1. Arnold writes: "Unless we find singleness of heart and mind, our dividedness will tear us to pieces" (p. 34). Why is this? Do you know anyone who is torn apart by inner dividedness?

2. If commitment to Christ is real, what kind of sacrifices might one have to be ready to make? Can you think of any scripture passages that speak to this? (See Lk. 9:23–27; 57–62; 2 Tim. 3:12; Phil. 3:7–11.)

3. Do commitment and trust preclude failure? Why not? How does Matthew 14:22–33 answer this?

4. Why is Jesus worthy to be trusted? Can you think of anything or anyone else who is worthy of our complete and total trust? Why not?

5. What is the key to overcoming fear? (See p. 72.) Have the group read 1 Jn. 4:16–18 and discuss why love is the key to overcoming fear.

6. Why might trust be the answer to life's perplexities, problems, and anxieties? Does Arnold mean to say that if you only trust in Jesus you won't have any questions or problems anymore?

Impact Questions

1. Christ wants us to give him our entire selves. How might you be holding back? Is there any way you might be divided in your heart? How so?

2. Where have you avoided sacrificing for Jesus? How might you be avoiding hardship for Christ?

3. When you are confronted with a problem or a worry, what is the first thing you do? Do you go immediately to Jesus, or do you do something else?

4. Instead of trusting, how have you been guilty of "puzzling too long about the difficult questions of faith" (p. 70)? What fruit is borne when such puzzling occurs?

5. Arnold writes: "It does not matter if we have enemies or what those enemies say about us" (p. 36). Can you honestly say this is true in your life? In what ways do you care too much about what others think?

Leader's Questions

_____

_____

_____

_____

_____

_____

_____

_____

_____

_____

Stretching Each Other

Augustine once said, "If Christ is not Lord of all, he is not Lord at all." Read Luke 9:18–27, 57–62 aloud. Jesus speaks to different people who live a divided, uncommitted life:

- those who are not willing to suffer for Christ (v. 24)

- those who want religion but who also want worldly success (v. 25)

- those who are afraid to stand publicly for Christ (v. 26)

- those who follow Christ so long as their physical needs are met (vv. 57–58)

- those who follow Christ as long as family obligations are met (vv. 59–60)

- those who profess Christ but are still emotionally bound to loved ones (vv. 61–62)

Have the group share in what category they fall or are most tempted to fall into. How so? Where is a lack of trust displayed? Remind the group of Arnold's words on p. 19: "Half-hearted Christianity is worse than no Christianity."

Going Forward

Like those in Luke 9:57–62, it is tempting to say one thing to Jesus but mean another. Encourage the group to spend time in quiet. Remind them what Arnold says on p. 70: "We must have an attitude of trusting dedication to Jesus that says, 'not my will, but Thy will' and makes us absolutely quiet inwardly."

Notes & Announcements

The Lower Nature

Part I

Preparing

The chapter addressing the lower nature is a very serious one. No one likes to think about sin. But overcoming sin and finding victory in temptation is central to the message of the Gospel. Following Christ is not just an ideology or a system of belief. It's about experiencing his power to change.

As you read this section (pp. 38–53), keep in mind the hope of the Gospel. God's judgment on sin is always a judgment of mercy. God accepts us just the way we are but loves us too much to let us stay the same. His love is a power that liberates us from sin. At times his mercy cuts like a knife. At other times it comforts and heals. The struggle against sin is always closely tied to the Cross, to the very love of God. It is here that sin is judged and sinners forgiven.

For further recommended reading: *Freedom From Sinful Thoughts,* by J. Heinrich Arnold (Plough).

Getting Started

Read the story from Plato entitled "Gygis' Ring" (Appendix D). The story raises the question, "Why be good?" In other words, if one had the power to do any evil or sinful act without anyone (even God) knowing about it, why refrain from doing so? Why not give into temptation, or sin a little, especially if no one would ever know?

Have the group discuss the question: "If you had access to Gygis' ring, why try to be good if you really don't have to?" What usually motivates people not to sin? In light of what Jesus says in the Sermon on the Mount (Mt. 5–7), what one thinks is as important as how one behaves. Why resist the "invisible" thoughts of evil that come into one's mind?

Studying Together

Focus Questions

1. What is the "lower nature?" Is it restricted to bodily appetites (i.e., to the physical level)? Or is it something more? How might the following verses help us understand "the flesh?"

   Gal. 6:16–21 — Rom. 8:5–8

   1 Jn. 2:15–17 — Eph. 2:1–3

2. Is temptation itself wrong or sinful? Why not?

3. Arnold asks, "Where does temptation end and sin begin" (p. 38)? How does he answer this? What does James 1:13–15 say about this? What do you think?

4. According to Arnold, what is the most essential thing in battling against sin and temptation? Why does the experience of Christ himself make all the difference?

5. There is sin from the lower nature and satanic sin. What is the difference between them?

Discovery Questions

1. Arnold emphasizes the fact that "Jesus was tempted just like any other human being" (p. 38). Why is this so important? Read Hebrews 2:14–18; 4:14–16. *(Note that Jesus came to not only forgive us our sin, but to save us from our sin.)*

2. Arnold claims that most people today live with burdened consciences. What do you think about that? What is a burdened

conscience like? Why is the conscience so important? How might it answer the question raised by the story of Gygis' Ring?

3. Why is admitting our sinful nature, acknowledging it for what it is, an important step in becoming liberated from it?

4. According to Arnold, what is or is not "of the world" is not always so easy to determine. There is no simple formula one can use to discern spirits. We cannot simply identify a list of outward things and then call them "worldly." Why is this? Why is discerning the "spirit of the world" the most important thing?

5. Arnold is uncompromising – there is no excuse for sin. There is no room for self-pity. Why?

Impact Questions

1. Think about the ways you might rationalize away or excuse your sin? Can you think of at least one way you do this?

2. Arnold asks: "Which of us takes our struggle with sin so seriously that we fight with loud cries and tears" (p. 43)? What area of temptation in your life do you need to take a more serious attitude toward? What will help make this different?

3. Arnold speaks about ideas, images, and thoughts that torment. Do you struggle with any? Can you share with the group or with someone you trust what they might be?

4. Arnold speaks about lovelessness as being the greatest sin (p. 51). How have you been too loveless, whether in thought, word, or deed?

5. Arnold claims that if we are ruled by *anything* but Christ we are living by the flesh (p. 48). Take an honest look at yourself and ask: Is there any thing, thought, activity, ability, person, goal, or pursuit that if taken away would throw you into despair or deep unhappiness? If there is, then maybe you are being ruled by something other than Christ.

Leader's Questions

_____

_____

_____

_____

_____

_____

_____

_____

_____

_____

Stretching Each Other

Arnold writes that if we tempt another person or bring another into temptation we sin. Think about some of the ways you could be guilty of this. *(Here are some ways we can easily tempt each other to sin: gossiping, flirting, being vain, boasting, using foul language, spending selfishly, boasting, watching impure images, being competitive, complaining, being too physical, talking idly, being cliquish, etc.)*

Have the group share how it can do better in helping each other overcome temptation. Try to get specific! Remember what Arnold says on p. 43: "we must not talk and preach to one another about love without recognizing that each one of us, too, is actually a sinner." As people share, they must not point fingers at one another. However, as Arnold says, "we must never be wishy-washy; out compassion must always be mixed with the salt of Christ" (p. 52).

Going Forward

Arnold writes a very comforting word when he says, "Even if we sink further and further into evil thoughts that we do not actually want,

God will see we do not want them, and he will help us" (p. 41). End your time in common praise. If different ones can testify to this, have them do so. Pray for those who are especially struggling in some area. Thank God for his help and for his continued forgiveness.

Notes & Announcements

_____

_____

_____

_____

_____

_____

_____

_____

The Lower Nature

Part II

Preparing

This session is tied very closely to the previous one. Keep in mind what was shared last week – especially what different participants said concerning the temptations they struggle with.

As you read this section (pp. 53–63), be especially open to God's voice. As a leader you are especially vulnerable to the sins of spiritual pride and false piety. Be honest about this and ask God's Spirit to show you any ways this might be true.

For further recommended reading: *Knowledge of the Holy,* by A.W. Tozer.

Getting Started:

Get a postcard-size picture that contains some (but not too much) interesting detail in it. Stand at the far end of the room and ask the group what it is they see. Ask them to describe it in as much detail as they can. Then move all the way forward so that the picture is just a few inches away from their eyes. Ask them to describe it again. Then go back to the far end of the room but move in a little closer. Keep going back and forth like this, modifying the distance so that it is less and less extreme. As you do this, keep asking the group what it is they see.

This little exercise is meant to illustrate that in looking at one's sin too closely (or not at all) one can quickly lose perspective, and even become confused. Remind the group that the topic of sin must always be considered in the larger perspective of who Christ is and what he accomplished. Only the Holy Spirit is able to help us see our sin for what it truly is.

Studying Together

Focus Questions

1. What kind of confession is Arnold writing about that helps us to become free of sin? How is it different from simply unloading on another?

2. Describe the sin of false piety. What other "self-sins" usually tag along with false piety?

3. Why is Arnold skeptical of psychology? Does this mean he is totally against it?

Discovery Questions

1. Why is pride the worst form of the flesh? What are the marks of pride?

2. Arnold writes: "The best way to experience nothing is to keep looking into yourself" (p. 60). Why do you think he says this? How has this been true in your own life?

3. There's a kind of paradox in what Arnold says. We are to take our personal sin seriously but not be overly preoccupied with it. What kind of self-judgment leads to God and what kind doesn't? How can one know the difference? How does 2 Cor. 7:8–13 help?

4. Do you agree or disagree with the following: "As long as you seek to be loved, you will never find peace. You will always find reasons for envy, but its real root is self-love" (p. 63). What kind of self-love is Arnold talking about? What is the answer to self-love? (Or, what does true love of self entail?)

5. Arnold writes: "Your way of judging people to be either great or insignificant, weak or strong, is completely unchristian" (p. 58). What else could you add to this list? (*e.g., gifted or ungifted, together or not together, etc.*) How is this kind of thinking marked by pride?

6. How can one's gifts, talents, and strengths be a greater hindrance to God than one's weaknesses? What does 2 Cor. 12:7–10 have to say about this? Can you cite any examples of how this might be true?

Impact Questions

1. Arnold writes: "Let us honor no one but God, and let us never accept honor for ourselves" (p. 60). Where have you given too much honor to another, and when have you taken too much honor for yourself?

2. In what ways have you been too inclined to watch yourself in the mirror?

3. In what ways are you trying to get others to love you? to recognize you? to pay attention to you? to admire you? Can you acknowledge these and turn from them?

4. How might you be trying to project an "image" or parade your "goodness" and "strengths" in front of others? Why is this? Can you see how this is a form of seeking power over others?

5. How might you be guilty of "looking at your brothers and sisters as if through a microscope" (p. 57)? What does Jesus have to say about this (Mt. 7:1–5)? What does a judgmental attitude really stem from? *(self-contempt)*

Leader's Questions

_____

_____

_____

_____

_____

_____

_____

_____

Stretching Each Other

Have the group individually write a letter of confession to God about something they especially feel convicted about from this study. Hand out a piece of paper and pencils and take enough time for each person in the group to write something. Maybe they need to find a quiet corner to do this. When they have finished have them fold the letter and put it in an envelope.

Once everyone is back together read James 5:16 out loud together. Then encourage each person to go to someone they trust, who walks with God, and share the contents of that letter to them. Sin hates to be in the light. Remind them, however, that when sin is confessed to a brother or sister in the assurance of God's forgiveness, it loses its grip and power.

Going Forward

End your time by focusing on Christ. Arnold says: "Don't look at yourself. Look to Christ" (p. 61). Christ is more important than our sin! Choose some songs together that focus on Christ, his character and his cause. Sing them together to close the session.

Notes & Announcements

_____

_____

_____

_____

_____

Reverence & Surrender

Preparing

In many respects, reverence and surrender are utterly foreign to our culture. We live in a increasingly vulgar society that not only cheapens but "rapes" what is holy. A sense of reverence is not only hard to come by but typically scorned. Anything and everything has become an object of ridicule or gossip.

The idea of surrender is even harder to swallow for many. Our age is thoroughly anti-authoritarian where all are "equalized" and assert their rights before the law. Personal autonomy, the freedom to choose, becoming your own person, and doing your own thing make it virtually impossible for people to surrender their lives to God or to one another.

For this reason, these two chapters can be difficult to grasp. Reverence for God and his creation, and surrendering to his will are more than mere acts. They are not concepts. They are, instead, deep experiences that grip a person's entire being. As you read these two chapters (pp. 73–81), keep this in mind. Also, ask God to show you the ways in which our "liberated" culture has adversely affected you. Come ready to confess the irreverence and resistance in your own life.

For further recommended reading: *The Imitation of Christ,* by Thomas á Kempis.

Getting Started

Begin by reading Isaiah 6:1–13 together. Ask the group how Isaiah's encounter with God relates to the chapters *Reverence* and *Surrender.*

How does Isaiah exhibit these two attitudes? How were reverence and surrender brought about?

Studying Together

Focus Questions

1. How does Arnold understand "reverence?" How is it related to but different from fear?

2. From what Arnold writes, how would you describe the person who properly fears God?

3. What does "surrender" entail? Describe the person who has surrendered himself totally to God?

4. What is necessary before a person can surrender to God?

Discovery Questions

1. Proverbs speaks a great deal about "the fear of God." Look at some of the following verses and discuss what this fear looks like (Proverbs 1:7; 8:13; 14:27; 15:16; 16:5–6; 23:17–18). What does a person gain when he fears God?

2. How does the fear of others negate or undermine the fear of God? Why do we tend to fear others more than God?

3. Why do we find it so difficult to surrender totally to God?

4. How might a reverence for God affect the way we worship? How would this reverence affect the way we relate to one another? to creation? to children?

5. Arnold speaks of misusing the name of God (p. 74). Besides the obvious, how might God's name get misused? How can "overusing" God's name express a lack of reverence?

6. Arnold speaks about our inclination to forget God (p. 74). Why? How does this relate to the question of reverence?

Impact Questions

1. As you read these two chapters, were you convicted about anything in particular? What?

2. Where have you been resistant in accepting the place Jesus has placed you? Are there any ways you might be appearing compliant on the outside but resistive on the inside (i.e., obedient but not surrendered)?

3. In what ways do you try to outshine your brother or sister so as to make an impression?

4. Are there any ways you are afraid to admit and show your weakness, either before God or before others?

Leader's Questions

_____

_____

_____

_____

_____

_____

_____

_____

_____

_____

Stretching Each Other

Arnold writes: "When a person has surrendered to God with heart and soul, he will then seek others in whom the same love is clearly expressed and surrender to them also" (p. 77). Discuss as a group how you can be more surrendered to one another. What is preventing you as a group from this greater surrender?

Going Forward

Remind the group that a lack of reverence and surrender toward each other is a spillover of a lack of reverence and surrender to God. Spend time in common prayer by having the group express to God their longing for a greater surrender and awe of him.

Notes & Announcements

_____

_____

_____

_____

_____

_____

_____

_____

Purity & Sincerity

Preparing

Purity and sincerity are all about the quality of our relationships – with God and each other. They are especially important with respect to the opposite sex. The lack of purity and genuineness between the sexes today has caused untold harm and anguish. As you read these two chapters (pp. 64–67, 82–85) especially think about how your relationships would be different if these two virtues were practiced.

Because some of the material in these chapters is sensitive in nature, it would be good to have the group (if it is mixed) divide up, with the men and women meeting separately. Before you meet together choose a person of the opposite sex to help you lead this session. Be sure he or she has a copy of this session in the Leader's Guide so that this person can properly prepare.

As you prepare, find a couple of photos that portray a man and woman together. These should be "typical." Especially look for advertising pieces. What you want is a photo that displays the impurity and superficiality of our age.

For further recommended reading: *A Plea for Purity: Sex, Marriage, and God,* by J. Christoph Arnold (Plough).

Getting Started

Begin by meeting together as a whole group. Explain that for this session the men and the women will meet separately. However, before the group divides have them discuss the values imbedded in the photo (or photos) you brought. Begin by sharing about the kind of values that are being communicated. More specifically, in what ways do the pictures reinforce impurity and insincerity? Do they have to be very explicit to have an impact? After a while, divide into your two groups.

Studying Together

Focus Questions

1. Keeping the content of these two chapters in mind, compare and contrast purity and sincerity. Do the same for impurity and insincerity. How are they different? How are they related?

Purity	Impurity
Sincerity	Insincerity

2. From what Arnold says about the German Youth Movement (pp. 83–84), list what it was they valued most.

Discovery Questions

1. For Arnold, is sexual impurity a matter of the flesh only? What else is involved? Is purity simply abstinence? How might the following scripture passage help us understand purity? (See Mt. 5:27–30; Tit. 1:15–16.)

2. Arnold's son, Johann Christoph, has written an entire book on the subject of purity entitled, *A Plea for Purity: Sex, Marriage, and God.* Concerning masturbation, he writes:

Masturbation can never bring true satisfaction. It is a solitary act. It is self-stimulation, self-gratification, self-abuse – it closes us within a dream world and separates us from genuine relationships. When it becomes habitual (which it often does), it aggravates isolation and loneliness. At its worst, as a breach in the bond of unity and love for which sex is created, it is comparable to adultery (p. 110).

3. Think about this honestly, and nondefensively. If you struggle in this area, what kind of fruit is born from masturbating? Is masturbation simply a harmless act? Does it bring you closer to others? Does it inspire love? What really motivates masturbation?

4. Arnold says that purity is a great blessing. Can you think of why that might be? What gifts accompany a pure life?

5. Arnold writes that "there is a danger of coming to an intellectual recognition of the truth and then living a life that conforms to it, when the truth is not yet actually given by God into our hearts and souls" (p. 82). What does he mean? Can you think of any examples?

6. Arnold argues that it is not "sinners" but those who use Christian words insincerely that are the worst enemies of God. What, exactly, does he mean by this? Why might this be so? (See Mt. 6:5–8; 7:15–23; 21:28–32; 1 Jn. 3:18.)

Impact Questions

1. Let's be honest. How do you specifically "play with impurity?" In your thought-life? Sexually? What you read and watch? How you dress? In your relationships? Are you willing to take up an attitude and repent? How are you going to assure that things will be different?

2. Arnold says that "it will be necessary to have a strong character and say 'No' to things which the general public approves of"

(p. 67). How do you let the "public spirit of our age" pressure you and cause you to compromise your conscience? What "images" do you need to battle against? What do you need to say "No!" to?

3. Arnold warns against "parrot-like religion." What does he mean by this? Can you cite any examples of parrotlike religion today? Do you see any of it in your own fellowship circles? What about in your own life?

4. What prevents you from being genuine? In what areas of your life do you use the right words without meaning them, or come across differently from the way you really are?

5. Where are you not being straightforward in your relationships or being two-faced about your true feelings? Why?

6. What are some of today's social conventions (in and outside the church) that mask facades, hypocrisy, or an ungenuine spirit? How do you participate in these?

Leader's Questions

_____

_____

_____

_____

_____

_____

_____

_____

_____

_____

_____

_____

_____

Stretching Each Other

While the two groups are still apart, have them discuss (without naming names) what the other group could do differently to help each other live a more pure and genuine life. Write these things down, clearly and specifically. Then each leader should exchange lists and read them to their respective groups. After this is done the groups should come back together to close the time.

Going Forward

Read Philippians 4:8–9 out loud. Then, in a time of common prayer, speak to God about those things that are true, noble, right, pure, lovely, admirable, excellent, and praiseworthy. Thank him for these things.

Notes & Announcements

_____

_____

_____

_____

_____

_____

_____

_____

The Church

Preparing

Most people have pretty strong feelings about the church. Before reading this chapter (pp. 89–95), examine your own feelings. Ask God to show you a new vision of what the church could and should be.

For further recommended reading: *The Authentic Witness,* by C. Norman Kraus

Getting Started

The image of the church that comes to most people's minds is a building. Some, however, think of an institution or a set of religious activities. Others think of a particular group of people. Whatever the conception, people have definite feelings about the church. Read the following two statements. Have the group express which one they feel best describes today's church. Which statement is the more accurate one? Why?

> Our world is drowning in a sea of sin. Though the church is our only ship of safety, sadly its hull is full of holes. If it wasn't for the storm outside, the stench inside would suffocate me to death.

> The Good News is that by grace we can live together in a new society where all relationships are being transformed and reconciled. This is exactly why the church is part of the Gospel. A new society, in the midst of the old, is possible!

Studying Together

Focus Questions

1. From what Arnold writes, describe his understanding of "the world." What are some adjectives he uses?

2. By contrast, how does Arnold describe the church? What are some of its characteristics? *(Note: Don't just look at some of the adjectives or metaphors he uses. Think about the implicit meaning in his use of terms. For example, the description "inner community" is rich in meaning.)*

3. To whom does the heavenly church come?

4. What happens when the Spirit of the Church comes to a group of people?

Discovery Questions

1. Why do you think Arnold is so adamant when he says, "We cannot say that the church is here or there" (p. 89). Do you think this is helpful?

2. Arnold says, "The fact that the church exists is the most important reality on earth" (p. 89). What do you think he means? Do you agree? (See Mt. 5:13 – 16; Jn. 13:34 – 35; 17:21; Eph. 1:22; 2:19 – 22; 1 Pet. 2:9 – 12.)

3. What is Arnold trying to get at with the metaphor of the lantern and the light (p. 91)? Why is this metaphor important?

4. What really holds a living church community together? Is this true today? What holds together many of today's churches?

5. Read 1 Cor. 12:12 – 27 together. Arnold refers to believers as being so united that they are like one body. Hence, each member should be willing to suffer for the other. Taking this metaphor of a body, discuss additional meanings it might have and how, if taken seriously, they would affect the church.

6. Arnold addresses the problem of "attachment to the culture" (p. 94). He refers to the Bruderhof – his own church commu-

nity – and the influences of European and German culture along with the Youth Movement.

a. Why might this be a problem? Why do you think he brings this up?

b. Is a given cultural background bad?

c. In what ways might today's church be too attached to the culture?

Impact Questions

1. Arnold asks some very probing questions on p. 95. Is this group, and the church to which it belongs, really showing something different to the world? How so? If not, why not?

2. Stanley Hauerwas, a contemporary Christian author, asks a similar question: "Can we so order our life in the church that the world might look at us and know that God is busy?" How could this group change so as to make God's presence a more visible reality to the world? What would need to become different for "the atmosphere of the Spirit of God to rule" (92)?

3. In what ways might we, as a group and as a church, be too smug toward ourselves – of having the attitude, "We are the church?"

4. The spirit of the world is a spirit of division. Is there any divisiveness among us? barriers? cliquishness? "class" distinctions?

Leader's Questions

_____

_____

_____

_____

_____

_____

_____

Stretching Each Other

Arnold writes: "Our time needs the tangible demonstration that God is stronger than all hate, all need, all sin, and all disunity" (p. 91). Brainstorm together about how to give a greater witness to this "tangible demonstration." Seek the Spirit's leading and choose one thing you can do as a group to show God's power over the world.

Going Forward

End your time together by detailing how to implement the above "tangible demonstration." Be concrete, practical, and clear as to what will happen, who will be involved, and what responsibilities need to be covered. Once this is done, thank God in prayer for the gift of each other and the unity he gives.

Notes & Announcements

_____

_____

_____

_____

_____

_____

_____

_____

Community

Preparing

The word "community" means different things to different people. Think about its different meanings. Make a list. As you read this chapter (pp. 96 – 105), keep in mind how Arnold uses the word "community."

For further recommended reading: *Why We Live in Community,* by Eberhard Arnold (Plough) and *Life Together,* by Dietrich Bonhoeffer (Harper).

Getting Started

Begin by reading Acts 4:32 – 35 together. Then have everyone empty their pockets – money, credit cards, check books, wallets, etc. – and place the contents in the center of the circle (or on a table up front). After this is done, have the group share their feelings about what they have just done. Then read Acts 2:42 – 47. What do you think the early Christians felt when they sold their possessions and goods? Why is it different today?

Studying Together

Focus Questions

1. Arnold seems to have a fairly specific idea of what community involves. How does he use the word? Describe his understanding of community.

2. How are Christian community and the Gospel related?

3. What needs to happen before one can have true community with others? What is the basis for Christian community?

Discovery Questions

1. Is "community," as sharing all things in common, an ethical ideal for Arnold? Why not? *(Note that for Arnold, community of goods is an outcome [not the foundation] of faith, the fruit [not the requirement] of full surrender to Christ.)*

2. Arnold cites several scripture passages that provide the rationale for "sharing all things in common" (p. 97). Look these up and study them carefully. Can you think of any other verses that support such radical sharing? (See Mk. 12:41–44; Mk. 10:28–31; Jn. 12:4–6; Acts 6:1–4; Rom. 15:25–28; 2 Thess. 3:11–13; Eph. 4:28.)

3. How does Arnold view wealth? How is wealth to be used?

4. As important as sharing is, what is the most decisive thing according to Arnold?

5. How important is commitment for building community with others? Is it good enough simply to be committed to people, or is there something more specific that needs to happen? Why might a specific group of people be important?

Impact Questions

1. What are some of the forces and factors today that hinder or obstruct the Spirit from gathering believers together like at Pentecost?

2. Like the psalmist (see Ps. 133) Arnold writes: "It is a great gift to live with brothers and sisters" (p. 101). In our society, most would balk at this. Can you imagine how community with fellow believers would be a blessing? How so?

3. Arnold quotes Mt 6:21: "Where your treasure is, there is you heart." Where does your treasure lie? Be honest! Take inventory of your treasure-chest. How are your energies, thoughts, time,

and money, spent? Do they build up God's kingdom – a shared life with others – or do they secure a little kingdom of one's own?

4. If someone were to look at your life from the "outside," would there be any indications that your treasures lie in heaven and not on earth?

5. Arnold writes in a letter that he understands how disappointing community can be. We can let each other down. Nevertheless, Arnold still wishes to prove his faithfulness to Jesus and to his brothers and sisters by gathering with them (p. 104). How have you experienced disappointment? Despite this, how can you more faithfully gather with others?

Leader's Questions

_____

_____

_____

_____

_____

_____

_____

_____

_____

_____

_____

_____

Stretching Each Other

Arnold speaks of the Gospel as the news that we can live together as brothers and sisters in peace, in full trust and love to one another (p. 98). As a group, share how this could be more fully realized among you.

Then, seek the Spirit to show you at least one concrete way how you as a group could express your love one for another.

As you seek together, remind the group of what Arnold writes on p. 104: "If we want to live in church community *we must do it for the sake of God alone.* Otherwise, even with the best will, we will be like parasites on the inner life of the church." In other words, true Christian fellowship is costly. It works on the basis of what we are willing to give, not what we hope to receive.

Going Forward

Spend some time in common prayer thanking God for the gift of each other. Thank God for specific things. Also spend some time in gathered silence, asking God to reveal to you the ways in which you – your lifestyle and priorities – do more "scattering" than "gathering."

When finished, have the group "take back" their wallets and possessions. In doing this, challenge them to consider ways to keep their "pockets" empty for the cause of Christ and for one another.

Notes & Announcements

_____

_____

_____

_____

_____

_____

_____

_____

Leadership & Gifts

Preparing

For the disciple of Jesus, leadership is not what the world deems it to be. True leadership has little to do with motivational strength, charisma, giftedness, or skill. Neither is it a matter of knowledge or training. Least of all does it have to do with position or power (Acts 4:13). Authentic leadership is all about serving and sacrificing. As you read (pp. 106–120), ask God to show you how you can more fully serve him and others.

For further recommended reading: *Community and Growth,* by Jean Vanier.

Getting Started

For each person in the group, write on a 3 x 5 card a talent, skill, or gift (e.g., writing, organization, cooking, math, building skills, teaching, cleanliness, physical strength, ability to listen, etc.). When the group gathers together give each one a card. Ask them the following question: "On your card is written a gift, skill, or talent. If you could choose a career based on that gift, skill, or talent, what would it be? Why?"

After sharing a bit, now ask the group to consider the following: "Imagine that as a group we have been given the task to found and run a children's home. Using your gift, skill, or talent listed on your card, what could do to help in this effort?"

The goal of this little activity is to bring to the group's attention the following: When left wide open and with no reference other than to oneself, we tend to think about our gifts and talents in terms of what will bring us personal fulfillment. In contrast, when given a task, or a common project or goal, we invariably think in terms of what we can contribute, and how we can work effectively with others. God gives each person different abilities and gifts, but he does so not for personal enjoyment *per se,* but for the benefit of others.

Studying Together

Focus Questions

1. How does Arnold describe a leader? What are the qualities of a true leader?

2. What kind of tension does a leader face? (See pp. 110–111.)

Arnold emphasizes love as the greatest gift. Find various passages in the book where he does this. Have different ones in the group read what Arnold has to say about the primacy of love.

Discovery Questions

1. Why, according to Arnold, is it such a terrible thing to use leadership as a position of power over others? Can you think of additional reasons beyond what Arnold writes?

2. Arnold says that there is no privilege in a servant of the Word's (pastor's) task. Why does he say this? How might a position of spiritual leadership be an extra burden to carry?

3. Arnold exclaims: "We denounce the honoring of men" (p. 112). Why does he say such a thing? In what sense does he mean this? Does he mean we ought never to honor others? (See Rom. 10:12; 13:7; 1 Cor. 12:23–24; Eph. 6:2.)

4. Why does Jesus give different gifts to his followers? (Also see 1 Cor. 12:7; 14:12, 26; Eph. 4:7–13.)

5. Why is a lack of giftedness unimportant in God's eyes? What is important? How might being "too gifted" be more of a problem than not having enough gifts?

6. Arnold argues that people speak too lightly about "being filled with the Spirit" (p. 117). What do you think he means by this? Do you agree? Can you think of any examples?

7. Arnold says, "We must be willing to sacrifice our natural talents for the sake of the whole Body" (p. 116). What does he mean? Can you share any examples of how this has been true in your life?

8. What is the gift of discernment? How is it to be exercised? How might it relate to Arnold's thoughts on the authority of leaders?

Impact Questions

1. Arnold argues that, "A true Christian church cannot be a living organism unless there is clear leadership" (p. 106). If this is the case, are there any ways you are resisting (or failing to support) the leadership of those over you? How?

2. Where might you be guilty of trying to exercise power over others? How have you been too pushy, or guilty of "correcting too much" (p. 117)?

3. Arnold warns against being bound by a leader and likewise of trying to bind others to oneself. Have you been (or are you now) guilty of this?

4. Envy is very destructive. Arnold especially mentions how terrible it is "to feel we have not been given our fair share; to feel that others have received more from God" (p. 115). Can anyone share how this might be a particular struggle? Is there any envy in the group?

Leader's Questions

_____

_____

_____

_____

_____

_____

_____

_____

_____

_____

Stretching Each Other

Go back to the activity you began with in "Getting Started." On the other side of the 3 x 5 card, have each person write down one talent, gift, or skill they have. Then discuss a project you could do together. After selecting a project, discuss specific ways each member can contribute, based on what they wrote down on their 3 x 5 card. Have the group choose someone to lead (take responsibility for) the project. Make sure that everyone contributes!

Going Forward

Close by reading the parable of the talents together (Mt. 25:14–30). Then spend time praying in response to the parable and to what was shared earlier.

Notes & Announcements

_____

_____

_____

_____

_____

_____

_____

Forgiveness & Baptism

Preparing

Forgiveness and baptism belong together. All too often, however, we separate them. When this happens, the result is the "spiritualizing" of forgiveness and the "ritualizing" of baptism. Forgiveness and baptism are very personal experiences. Yet as personal as they are, they are not private. True forgiveness and living baptism affect our relationships with others. As you read these two chapters (pp. 121–127, 141–146), note the ways in which they are related. Reflect on how our relationship with God and how our relationships with others are bound together.

For further recommended reading: *Seventy Times Seven: Stories of Forgiveness,* by J. Christoph Arnold (Plough).

Getting Started

Make a visual aid large enough for the group to see. It should look like a score card. On it you should have two separate lists: (1) Thou Shalt Nots; (2) Thou Shalts. Then in two columns you should have the following: (1) What I've done; (2) What I've failed to do.

Ask the group to imagine that God has such a moral score card for each person. Have them imagine what their score sheet would look like. Arbitrarily mark the sheet you have. Then ask them to share their feelings. Use this to illustrate how living under such a code is like living under the Law of the Old Covenant (Gal. 2:15–16).

Then read Colossians 2:13–14. Ask them to consider how with Christ this moral score card changes. Let them share their response. Then show them that Christ not only erases the score card (i.e., wipes the slate clean), but nails it to the Cross (destroys it altogether). Tack the sheet of paper to a wooden cross. Explain how that in Christ, God no longer relates to us on the basis of keeping the law. Our life is now hidden in Christ (Col. 3:3).

Studying Together

Focus Questions

1. What conditions must be met before true forgiveness from God can be had? Can you list some of them?

2. What kinds of things cause the door to God to be closed?

3. What does Arnold mean by baptism? What is its purpose? Make a list of what baptism includes. Is baptism simply a personal, private act?

4. What does baptism accomplish? Why is baptism a gift?

Discovery Questions

1. Arnold says that "the only way to find inner peace in Christ is through peace with one's brothers" (p. 121). Why? Do you agree?

2. Read the following scripture passages: Mt. 5: 23 – 24; 6: 14–15; 18:21–35. How important is forgiving others in experiencing God's forgiveness?

3. What does Arnold mean when he says: "It is not enough to seek peace for ourselves, for our own souls" (p. 125)?

4. How is baptism a fitting symbol of God's forgiveness? Is forgiveness a "state" or is it a "power?"

5. Why does Arnold argue that "it is better to remain unbaptized than to take the step halfheartedly…" (p. 143)? How serious is the step of baptism? What makes it so serious?

6. How might baptism symbolize a new beginning? Does baptism mean the end of sin and temptation?

7. Read Romans 6 together. What does it mean that we are no longer slaves to sin? Does this mean perfection?

8. What do you think Arnold means when he says, "Baptism is the declaration of a good conscience before God" (p. 140)? How does one obtain a clear conscience? (See 1 Jn. 1:9; Jas. 5:16.)

Impact Questions

1. Arnold claims that "God hears only those who forgive" (p. 126). Are you by chance harboring any unforgiveness, resentment, bitterness, or anything else against another person? Are you willing to forgive?

2. Arnold encourages us to "look at one another with new eyes and see each other as a gift from God" (p. 125). What kinds of things would help this to happen in your life? Who do you need to look at with new eyes?

3. Arnold writes, "We must experience what it means to be burdened with sin *and then freed"* (p. 124). Has this ever happened in your life?

4. Baptism is a covenant with God *and* with others. What kind of church does a fellowship of Christians need to be to take baptism seriously? Does our fellowship have the kind of covenant with each other to make baptism a reality for everyday life?

Leader's Questions

_____

_____

_____

_____

_____

_____

_____

Stretching Each Other

Return to the visual aid with the score card on it. Have the group share where they have been guilty of keeping a score card against another person. How has this "score sheet" divided them? Are they willing to nail it to the Cross, like Jesus did when he died for us? Pass around a sheet of paper. Ask the group to write down the mental score sheet they have been using against this other person. Have them name the specific judgments they have been making. Then have them come up and tack it to the wooden cross.

Remind the group that if there is a conflict they should go directly to the other person to clear it up. They should seek the help of others if they have already tried this. (See Mt. 18:15–20.)

Going Forward

End the time together in quiet by having the group reflect on the following question: "Is there anything hindering you from taking the step of baptism?" For those who have been baptized, ask: "In what ways have you failed to live according to your baptism vows?"

Notes & Announcements

_____

_____

_____

_____

_____

_____

_____

_____

Unity & The Lord's Supper

Preparing

Most people do not think of the Lord's supper as a meal of unity. As you read these two chapters (pp. 128–133, 147–150), think about how Jesus' prayer for unity and the Lord Supper go together. Pay particular attention to the kind of unity Arnold is referring to.

Getting Started

Ask the group to think of a way where each person in the group is in a sitting position, at the same time, and without the use of any chairs or other manmade objects *(The idea is to get the group to form a circle and have them sit down on each other's laps. This can only be done if it is done together and at the same time. Separate men from women.)*

The point of this activity is to help the group experience the work, nature, and joy of being united. Throughout this session, you will want to refer back to this activity to illustrate the different aspects of unity *(e.g., interdependency, a common goal, cooperation, including everyone, etc).*

For further recommended reading: *Love to Christ and Love to the Brothers,* by Eberhard Arnold (Plough).

Studying Together

Focus Questions

1. On what basis is true unity possible? What has to happen before a group becomes united heart, soul, and mind?

2. What does real unity involve? How does Arnold describe a united fellowship of believers? Can you think of other ways to describe unity?

3. Arnold describes the Lord's Supper as "a meal of unity" (p. 147). Aside from its religious significance, how does a meal symbolize unity? Reflect on Arnold's reference to the grain of wheat and the grapes. What does this metaphor suggest?

4. In addition to symbolizing unity, what else is the Lord's Supper a symbol of?

Discovery Questions

1. Why do you think unity is so important to Arnold? What are some of the biblical reasons for unity's importance? (See Mt. 12:30; Jn. 17:21ff; Eph. 1:9–10; 4:3–16; Phil. 2:1–5.)

2. Do you agree with Arnold that God "says the same thing to all, also in practical matters" (p. 129)? If this is true, then is majority opinion a valid way for God's people to make decisions? (See Acts 15.)

3. What kinds of things undermine unity in a group? Arnold lists several things in our culture which lead to disintegration and separation (p. 132–133). Can you add to this list? What forces in our society, in the church, and in each person prevent a brotherhood of unity from happening?

4. What dangers exist when unity is lacking among a people?

5. What happens when the Lord's Supper is taken wrongly? (See 1 Cor. 11:17ff.)

6. What should we do before we come to the Lord's Table? As we come to it, what should our posture be?

7. Wherein lies the real presence (or sacramental reality) of Christ: in the elements or the participants?

Impact Questions

1. In what ways have you tried to shake hands over fences and barriers that still remain, of resolving differences by making concessions? Be honest!

2. Arnold says: "Standing for God always has a unifying power" (p. 128). Is this true in your life? Are you a gatherer or a scatterer?

3. Similarly, Arnold writes: "Where there is true expectation, people are usually drawn together" (p. 128). Share how this has been true in your life.

4. Assessing our group, do we have the kind of expectation that is necessary to draw us closer together? Are we growing in unity? How? If not, why not?

5. In partaking of the Meal, Arnold says we should be ready to sacrifice our life – in fact *should* sacrifice our life – like Jesus (p. 148). Is your life in Christ a sacrifice? Is there anything you can change to express your readiness to sacrifice or die for Jesus?

Leader's Questions

_____

_____

_____

_____

_____

_____

_____

_____

_____

_____

Stretching Each Other

Arnold writes: "Let us pray that we may be gathered together with all those who live in expectation of him" (p. 128). Discuss as a group ways you can express your longing for greater unity in the body of Christ. Ask the Spirit to guide you in choosing one activity that expresses this longing for more unity. Decide what that might be and determine how and when to do it.

Going Forward

Spend time in common prayer asking God to lead the group in this. If appropriate, share in the Lord's Supper together. At the very least, share a good meal together.

Notes & Announcements

Church Discipline

Preparing

This topic is virtually unheard of, much less discussed, in today's contemporary church. Unfortunately, because of certain abuses, "church discipline" has become taboo. For Arnold, however, when properly applied and rightly received, it is a great gift. As you read (pp. 134–140) be aware of any biases or misgivings you might have on the subject of discipline. Ask God to open your heart to the true meaning of church discipline.

For further recommended reading: *Confessing Your Sins to One Another*, by John R. Stott.

Getting Started

Have the group respond to the following: "When I think about the times my parents disciplined me I feel _____." Have them share why this is so.

After everyone has had a chance to share, explain to them how easy it is for us to subconsciously project the feelings of our past – especially toward our parents – onto God. The subject of church discipline is a delicate and difficult one partly because the word "discipline" has such negative connotations. As you discuss this chapter, remind the group that God is the perfect father and his will for church discipline arises from his perfect and holy love.

Studying Together

Focus Questions

1. A number of scripture passages are referred to on page 134 regarding the basis of church discipline. Read them together. What common themes emerge?

2. What, exactly, is the purpose of church discipline?

3. In what spirit should church discipline be administered?

4. Is every sin to be disciplined or treated in the same way? Why not?

Discovery Questions

1. If properly administered and rightly received, how is church discipline a blessing?

2. Arnold says, "We cannot excuse evil by saying that where there is wheat there is always chaff" (p. 137). What are some other typical excuses we have today for not confronting sin seriously in the church?

3. Arnold says that "we must have deep respect and reverence for those who are disciplined" (p. 136). Why? Shouldn't they just be shunned?

4. How might discipline, forgiveness, and reconciliation be tied together?

5. Arnold argues that in a dead church, discipline is all but ignored (p. 137). How might this be?

6. Arnold emphasizes the importance of "giving ourselves completely to Jesus" when undergoing church discipline (p. 138). Why do you think this should be the focus? *(Note the temptation to get locked on one's sin is totally destructive.)*

7. Referring to Mt. 16:19, Arnold writes: "the forgiveness of sin is connected with the church...Forgiveness is not a private matter"

(pp. 139–140). What does this mean? Why is the church, in particular, important in matters of discipline?

Impact Questions

1. Arnold is clear that church discipline is based wholly on the words of Jesus as found in Mt. 18:15–20. Read this passage. As a group, are you willing to agree to or abide by this passage? If you are, what will this mean? What kind of covenant will you need to make with each other in order for Matthew 18 to come alive?

Depending on the commitment level of your group, have the group give each other honest feedback on the remaining questions. If the group can agree to it, as each person shares let others in the group share what they think towards that person and what they are saying.

2. Arnold warns against falling into extremes (pp. 138–139). How have you failed to exercise the balance between love and truth? Where have you been "too polite" or "too harsh"?

3. Arnold warns against making "general accusations." Instead, specifics should be brought to a person's attention (p. 139). How have you failed in this? Where have you dropped comments or said things in a general way instead of specifically going to the person or addressing the specific problem at hand?

4. "If someone speaks plainly to us," Arnold says, "we must not be touchy" (p. 139). In what ways are you touchy or defensive? Do you listen when someone approaches you about a problem, or do you immediately try to argue your side?

Leader's Notes

_____

_____

_____

_____

_____

_____

_____

_____

_____

_____

Stretching Each Other

As noted earlier, Arnold says: "We cannot excuse evil by saying that where there is wheat there is always chaff" (p. 137). Discuss ways in which you have been making excuses with each other. Is there anything in the group or dynamic of the group that displeases Jesus? Be specific.

Perhaps different ones might need to take some time away from the group so as to gain greater clarity on how far they have gone off. Remember what Arnold says: "Discipline is carried out only at the request of the person concerned" (p. 134). Remember too, that as a group all share in the guilt – even if some individuals share a greater guilt. In this sense, therefore, Arnold writes: "We must have deep respect and reverence for those who are disciplined."

If different ones need to take some time away, you as the leader need to make sure that they are well loved during this time. Designate a person or couple who will make an extra effort to visit them. The church is never to do the judging; only God can do this. *(Do not let this time away from the group go on too long. Restore the person or couple as soon as you and they feel that God has brought about a real change.)*

Going Forward

Before closing, those who have asked to take a distance from the group should leave. If no one feels the need to do this, discern whether or not to close your time in prayer. If you decide to pray, do so in the sense of asking God's forgiveness for wherever there has been failure. Also, pray for those who especially feel their guilt. Don't forget to thank God for his forgiveness and for the possibility of a new beginning.

Notes & Announcements

_____

_____

_____

_____

_____

_____

_____

Love & Marriage

Preparing

Too often the traditional view of marriage and of love is viewed as out-moded and restrictive. As you read this chapter (pp. 151–168) pay special attention to its many blessings. Ask yourself how things would be different if people were to apply Arnold's words seriously.

In preparing, think especially about your group. Not all the questions below will be appropriate to ask or discuss in your group. Pray for discernment as you get ready to lead this session. Be prepared with some questions of your own.

For further reading: *A Plea for Purity: Sex, Marriage, and God,* by J. Christoph Arnold (Plough).

Getting Started

The week before you meet together for this session, select three people to prepare a mock debate of which you will be the moderator. On one end of the spectrum is the extreme *Fundamentalist Position* which has a very negative, restrictive, fearful, legalistic, attitude toward sex. Even in marriage, sex is not to be overly enjoyed since its main function is pro-creation. This position argues that the ideal Christian state is celibacy, and marriage is a necessary accommodation to humanity's sinful condi-tion. The husband has final authority over his wife since women are weaker and more prone to be misled.

At the other end of the spectrum is the extreme *Liberated Position* which argues that sex can be enjoyed with whomever as long as there is care, tenderness, and mutual consent. This position believes that the traditional restrictions were necessary due to natural constraints, but now that we have effective means for birth-control, there is no fundamental reason why one has to restrict sex to marriage. What God created is natural and all that really matters to God is that there is love. Husbands and wives share equal power and as such role distinctions are unimportant.

In the middle lies the *Sacramental Position* which believes that love, sex, and marriage are sacred. This is the position that Arnold seeks to articulate. Sex is not only good, but to be enjoyed, as long as it is in a marriage relationship based on faith and lifelong faithfulness. Though the body is not to be despised, its impulses are to be submitted to God's order and will. Husbands and wives are different yet complement one another. Authority lies in the unity that exists between husband and wife, not in roles or arrangements of power.

Have these three folks do a bit of preparation based on their respective positions. Some questions to ask to get the debate going are: (1) Is it wrong to have sex outside of marriage? (2) What's the purpose of sex anyway? (3) What is the basis and purpose of marriage? Is a lifetime commitment important? Why? Why not? (4) What's wrong with young people getting physically intimate, as long as it doesn't go too far? (5) When there's a dispute between a couple or a big decision to be made, who should decide?

Start your time moderating this mock debate. Use it to get the wheels turning before you turn to the contents of the book. Keep the debate away from a lot of joking. It doesn't need to be overly serious, but neither should it become irreverent. After you finish the debate, ask the group to discuss which position best fits with what Arnold writes.

Note: If you have a youth group, this session would be an especially good one to invite parents to. Get them involved as much as you can. Depending on the length of the debate, you may want to take two weeks to do this session.

Studying Together

Focus Questions

1. What are some adjectives you would use to describe Arnold's view of sex?

2. What should be the determining factor in a serious relationship leading toward marriage? What should a marriage relationship be based on anyway?

3. What does a healthy marriage include? What kind of unity should exist between a married couple?

4. What are some of the factors and forces that can either destroy the marriage bond or lead a couple apart?

5. How would you describe Arnold's view of singleness? Is it overly optimistic or idealistic?

Discovery Questions

1. Why is physical and emotional attraction insufficient to base a relationship on?

2. Why is sex sacred? Why does it belong to marriage alone? How might it relate to God's image? Discuss some of the reasons why one should wait until marriage before engaging in sexual intimacy. What scripture passages speak to this? (See Gen. 2:24; Mt. 19:6–9; Heb. 13:4; 1 Cor. 6:15–20; Mt. 5:27–30; Eph. 5:1–6.)

3. Arnold says: "Having a marriage certificate does not give one the freedom to live for the body and its appetites" (p. 157). What should motivate sexual love between a husband and wife?

4. Arnold emphasizes that a serious relationship should lead two people closer to Jesus. In fact, he says that marriage "should double our dedication to Jesus, not weaken it" (p. 157). What kind of fruit will there be to indicate that a relationship is centered in Christ?

5. Arnold refers to the man's task as representing Christ as the head and the woman's task to represent Jesus as the Body (pp. 155–156). How is this an apt metaphor between husband and wife? How does this speak to their respective roles?

6. How might marriage, as wonderful a gift as it is, absorb our love in the wrong way (p. 167)?

7. Arnold takes Jesus' words about divorce and remarriage very seriously. (See Mt. 5:27–32; 19:6.) Without getting into a lengthy discussion on this particular topic, what are some of the reasons why lifelong faithfulness is God's ideal? *(Note Christ's relationship to the Church and God's faithful, unwavering, long-suffering love toward his people. Marriage is but a dim reflection of God's constancy and faithfulness.)*

Impact Questions

At this point, you will want to break into two groups with men and women being separate. You will also want to give married couples, if there are any, opportunities to discuss some of these questions separately.

1. What strikes your heart or conscience most after reading this chapter?

2. Arnold writes that we should not let our feelings of affection move casually from one person to another (p. 152). Why? What's wrong with having feelings? In what ways have you been struggling with this?

3. Arnold says that God's blessing is on any couple where unity is experienced in the right order (p. 155). Are there any ways you have gone against this order? Where in your marriage is God's order being ignored?

4. Arnold describes sex under God's order as being "an awe-inspiring, mysterious, noble, chaste, and peaceful act" (p. 164). Is this true in your marriage? Why not?

5. If you are in a committed relationship with another person, share with each other where you have failed to have a humble and open heart.

6. How might you be clinging too much to marriage? What is Arnold's answer to the unfulfilled longing to get married?

Leader's Questions

_____

_____

_____

_____

_____

_____

_____

_____

_____

_____

_____

Stretching Each Other

Discuss the idea of making a covenant of sexual purity – outside and within marriage. Have the group articulate a short but decisive pledge. For those who are married, highlight the significance of God's order. In other words, will couples pledge not to pressure each other sexually but instead to make unity of spirit and heart a higher priority?

Going Forward

Arnold writes: "There is nothing that surpasses the inner warmth, tenderness, and fruitfulness of unity with Jesus. This…can fill any void" (p. 166). End your time in worship focusing on your betrothal to Jesus.

Notes & Announcements

_____

_____

_____

_____

_____

_____

_____

_____

Family Life

Preparing

Parents, adults, and young people can all benefit from this chapter (pp. 169–187). What you choose to emphasize will depend greatly on the make-up of your group. As you prepare, pay special attention to those sections that are particularly relevant to your group.

For further recommended reading: *A Little Child Shall Lead Them: Hopeful Parenting in a Confused World,* by J. Christoph Arnold (Plough/IVP).

Getting Started

Ask the group to think quietly to themselves of different qualities that characterize a childlike spirit (the qualities of being a child). Then ask different ones to get up and silently act out a particular quality of child-likeness. If individuals are too bashful, encourage them to partner up. Keep a list of the different qualities that get acted out.

Point out how important children are in this chapter. Note that this chapter begins not with a discussion of parents, and their tasks, but with children.

Studying Together

Focus Questions

1. Find those sections in the chapter that emphasize the significance of children and the importance of a childlike spirit. Have different ones read these sections out loud.

2. What are characteristics or experiences that come more naturally to children?

3. What kind of discipline does a child need most and respond to best?

4. What happens when parents are too soft on their children?

Discovery Questions

1. Arnold speaks of having a reverence for children and leading them to have reverence for their parents. What does he mean by this? Why is reverence so important?

2. What is the best way to lead a child to God? What should a parent or teacher avoid in this endeavor? Can you think of examples beyond those mentioned by Arnold, of how parents can put religious pressure on their children? What is "religious pressure?"

3. Arnold speaks about being wary of extremes (p. 173). What do you think he means by this? Can you think of other extremes than the ones he mentions?

4. Arnold writes: "We fail our children when our emotional feelings and ties push us around" (p. 174). What does he mean? What might Arnold mean when he refers to "emotionalism" (p. 185) and "emotional ties that bind" (p. 186)? Can you cite any examples of this in your life, especially in your family? Why is this so destructive?

5. Why isn't it very good to over-explain the important mysteries of life to children? What *is* most important for them to know?

6. When children sin or play with indecencies, what does Arnold suggest we do? What mustn't we do?

7. Why is it important to recognize that "children differ in how they learn" (p. 178). In what ways does our society put undo emphasis upon academics?

Impact Questions

1. How can you become more childlike? What forces in our culture make it difficult for you to have a childlike spirit?

2. Where have you failed to show reverence, either to your parents or to the children in your care?

3. Arnold writes: "We must love our children so much that we are ready to fight for their souls" (p. 173)? How have you failed to engage in this fight (or given up the fight altogether)?

4. Arnold says that a "certain sharpness toward children is healthy, but *impatience* is not" (p. 174). What does he mean by this? How does one know when a spirit of impatience begins to creep in? Are there any ways you can become more patient with the children in your care?

Have the group give each other honest feedback on the remaining questions. As each person shares let others in the group respond.

5. Do your children, or the ones in your care, doubt what you say (p. 175)? Why? Do you follow through with your word, especially in matters of discipline?

6. What indications are there, if any, that you are too emotionally tied to your parents or that your children are too emotionally tied to you? Can you be specific?

7. Are there any ways you may be putting religious pressure on your children?

Leader's Questions

_____

_____

_____

_____

_____

_____

_____

_____

_____

_____

Stretching Each Other

As Arnold points out, children have tremendous significance in the eyes of Jesus. Therefore, they should be a priority in our lives. Children also instinctively respond to adults whom they trust. Ask each person in the group to pick one child in their life with whom they can build a deeper relationship of trust. Have them reflect on one concrete thing they can do toward this end. Have different ones share their idea, and then have the group offer honest, helpful feedback.

Periodically, as the group continues to meet together, ask them how this relationship is going.

Going Forward

End your time together in intercessory prayer. Have the group pray for the different children in their lives.

Notes & Announcements

_____

_____

_____

_____

_____

_____

_____

Illness & Death

Preparing

No one likes to talk about death – especially their own. Yet each one of us if fully aware of our own mortality. Our culture has very little capacity to deal with sickness, let alone face suffering or death. As you read this chapter (pp. 188–196), ask God to show you the ways in which you avoid questions of death and suffering. Try to become more aware of your attitude toward illness and any fears you may have toward death.

For further recommended reading: *I Tell You A Mystery: Life, Death, and Eternity,* by J. Christoph Arnold (Plough).

Getting Started

Collect a variety of journals, magazines, and newspapers (Christian and secular). Have the group look at them with the following question in mind: "Find pictures and phrases that typically express our culture's fear (or avoidance) of sickness, pain, and death. Cut/tear them out and be ready to share with the group what you come up with." As each picture is shown, pin or glue it up on some kind of poster/bulletin board.

The point of this activity is to get the group to articulate their own feelings about illness, suffering and dying. These are not easy subjects to discuss openly. Be aware of this as you seek to guide this session.

Studying Together

Focus Questions

1. How would you describe Arnold's general attitude toward illness and death? *(positive or negative? fearful or accepting? etc...)*

2. When we are sick or faced with the prospect of dying, what should we do?

3. When there is illness or the question of death, when is Christ able to do his work most?

Discovery Questions

1. Arnold speaks of the following paradox: "All sickness is a form of evil, yet we must accept it as from God's hand" (p. 188). Notice what he does not say. He does not say that all sickness *is* evil, nor that sickness is willed by God. What do you think he means?

2. There are other paradoxes in this chapter. Can you point them out? *(Note the following: Death is an enemy, yet is also means closeness to Jesus – p. 193; it's understandable to fear death but in Jesus all fears vanish – pp. 188–189; what finally counts in our relationship to God, yet love to God cannot be separated from love to other's – p. 195; that children have to suffer is very strange, yet the suffering of the innocent always has great significance for the church – p. 196.)* Share about these paradoxes and their meaning.

3. What does true healing entail? Though God often wills to heal the body, what is his ultimate will when it comes to physical suffering? (See Jn. 9:1–12; Rom. 8:28–29; Lk. 17:11–19; Jas. 5:14–16; 2 Cor. 4:16–18)

4. Arnold speaks of "the fulfillment of a dedicated life" (p. 189) and how vital this is in preparing for eternity. What do you think he means by this? Why is this important? (See Phil. 1:19–26; 1 Cor. 15:55–58; 1 Jn. 16-18; 1 Tim. 6:11–12.)

5. Arnold writes: "Pain deepens something in one's heart and life" (p. 191). What do you think he means by this? Can you share some examples of how this is so?

6. Death is more than cessation. What else is it according to Arnold? Why is this so important to remember?

7. What are your thoughts with regard to Arnold's answer to the question of praying for someone who has died? What do you think about this question? Are there any other relevant scripture passages that might address this question? (See Heb. 9:26–28; 1 Pet. 3:18–20.)

Impact Questions

1. Arnold writes: "All of us should live life so as to be able to face eternity at any time" (p. 188). Is your life plowing ground for eternity, or is it being lived only for what is temporary?

2. If "this earth in not yet fully our home" (p. 193), then what kinds of things can we do now to demonstrate that we have a greater, nobler destiny?

3. Think about the meaning of Jesus' promise in John 14:2: "I am going to prepare a place for you." Why is the metaphor of a house with many rooms such a comfort? Imagine together the mystery of this place.

4. Arnold writes that "the suffering of an innocent child always has great significance for the church" (p. 196). If any are able and willing to share, have them tell about their own experience of how this is true.

Leader's Questions

_____

_____

_____

_____

_____

_____

_____

_____

_____

_____

Stretching Each Other

Have the group find or draw pictures/symbols that express their faith in God's goodness and in his future. Perhaps certain scripture passages could also be written down. Then pin or glue them on top of those pictures that were pinned up earlier.

Going Forward

Read John 14 out loud together to close your time with. Then let the group respond as they feel led. Allow time for quiet. It is likely that some in the group will be feeling the loss of a loved one. Maybe some are facing the presence of suffering and death in their lives.

Notes & Announcements

_____

_____

_____

_____

_____

_____

_____

Evil, Darkness, & the Fight

Preparing

These two chapters (pp. 197–216) address a very serious subject. On the one hand, very few people take evil or the struggle between good and evil seriously today. On the other hand, those who do pay attention to evil, unfortunately, border on a fascination with it. As you prepare for this week's study, bear in mind what Paul writes in Eph. 6:10–18. Read and meditate on this passage. Ask God to show you specific ways you can put on the full armor of God.

Because of the amount of material covered in these two chapters, you may wish to take two weeks to do this session.

For further recommended reading: *Thy Kingdom Come: A Blumhardt Reader,* by Vernard Eller (Plough).

Getting Started

Arnold begins this chapter claiming that "many people either belittle evil or don't believe it exists at all." Have the group discuss how this might be so. On a large poster board, list the ways our society belittles or ignores evil's existence.

Evil Belittled	Evil Ignored

Studying Together

Focus Questions

1. What are some of Arnold's reasons for taking evil's power so seriously?

2. From what Arnold writes, describe the nature and influence of evil and of the demonic sphere. Is evil a spiritual-invisible force only or is there something more to it?

3. Where does Satan center his attack most? (See p. 202, 208)

4. Describe the church that is burning with its first love.

Discovery Questions

1. According to Arnold, "Why couldn't God forgive sin without the sacrifice of Jesus?" What does the Cross tell you about the nature of evil?

2. Arnold claims that "a true Christian should be a child toward evil and have no experience in its secrets" (p. 197). What do you think he means by this? Why is this? (See Rom. 12:9; 16:19 – 20; 2 Cor. 6:14.)

3. Why does Arnold pray for God's judgment (p. 199)? Isn't it mercy we need most? How is God's judgment a good thing?

4. When we deliberately commit a sinful act, what happens? (*We give room to an evil demon in our own life and surroundings p. 201. Don't forget that evil is any force or influence that is both independent of, yet an enslaving power over the will.*)

5. According to Arnold, what does it mean for the church to be salt. When does a church lose its saltiness?

6. Why do you think Arnold emphasizes the fact that Jesus didn't bring a new philosophy or a new religion?

7. As frightening as evil is, Arnold reminds us that in Jesus there is a greater Power (p. 202). What are some scripture passages that testify to Jesus' authority, power, and victory over evil? (See Mk.

14:62; Mt. 16:18; Jn. 14:30; Lk. 12:4–5; Jn. 16:11; Eph. 1:19–23; Col. 2:15; 1 Jn. 4:4.)

Impact Questions

1. In rejecting any form of contact with the demonic, Arnold rejects even the most "harmless" forms of spiritualism (p. 199). How do people dabble in the demonic today? How have (or do) you?

2. Arnold speaks of how Nazi Germany was ruled by evil spiritual powers or demons (p. 198). He also speaks of "the demonic net" that covers the earth. How might our own country be ruled by evil powers? Name those powers and forces that seem to have a collective stronghold over our culture. How would you describe the "net" that covers our nation? *(Remind the group that evil's primary intent is to separate us from God, from each other, and to divide us from ourselves. Have them think about the influences that divide and isolate people.)*

3. Are there any evil strongholds that are peculiar or especially strong in our city/town?

4. To get more specific, what strongholds do you personally have to battle against? Think about the dominant atmosphere(s) in which you live and function. *(e.g., family, work, school, neighborhood, living space, places of leisure & recreation, etc.)* What forces seek to bind and alienate people from God and from each other?

5. Arnold writes to a person whose fearful thoughts have gained too much power. Do you have any such thoughts? Can you share what they are?

6. Arnold protests against the idea that it is wrong to react when God's will is attacked. How well do you put up a fight when God's Kingdom is attacked? Do you speak out against sin and evil?

Leader's Questions

_____

_____

_____

_____

_____

_____

_____

_____

_____

_____

_____

Stretching Each Other

Satan is especially active in attacking the church (p. 204). Are there any satanic footholds in your (our) church or group that need exposing? Can we get specific? Read the Covenant of the Lord's Supper (pp. 214–216) together. Use this as a guide to evaluate the atmosphere of your own group and church.

As a group, are their any rock-bottom covenants we can make regarding "The Fight?" Discuss together any declarations of war you as a group feel compelled to make.

Going Forward

Arnold writes about the light of God's judgment breaking in and the rending of Satan's demonic net. Read Eph. 6:10–18 together. Spend time in common prayer asking God to expose this world's darkness. Name the specific strongholds and implore the Spirit's help in taking up the sword to rend this awful net. Pray also for those who shared about particular fearful thoughts that have gained too much power.

Notes & Announcements

_____

_____

_____

_____

_____

_____

_____

_____

World Suffering

Preparing

World suffering is everywhere. No nation, not even the most highly developed, is exempt from it. It is perhaps the suffering of the world that is of uppermost concern for many of today's world religions – including Christianity. Increasingly, people are turning to religion for answers and solutions. As you read this chapter (pp. 217–225), pay careful attention to Arnold's emphasis upon love. Reflect on this, especially in the light of 1 Cor. 13:1–3.

For further recommended reading: *The Individual & World Need,* by Eberhard Arnold (Plough).

Getting Started

Begin by having the group share their response to the following open question: "When I think of all the suffering and need in the world, what disturbs me most is _____." *(Responses might include: poverty, abortion, hunger, war, racial division, homelessness, starvation, family breakdown, overpopulation, ecological destruction, isolation, oppression, hatred, isolation, crime, injustice, etc.)*

Have the group share why they find this so disturbing. Keep in mind Arnold's distinction between sin and suffering. Various responses will fall into one or the other of these categories.

Studying Together

Focus Questions

1. This chapter is obviously about the tremendous suffering in the world. Besides this theme, what else does Arnold speak about?

2. Describe Arnold's view of political involvement and social protest. What place do these have? How important are they in his mind?

3. Arnold urges us to do more in the way of addressing the practical needs of others. Yet in reaching out, what is the most important thing? *(Read 1 Cor. 13:1–3 and discuss why love, not just good works, is the most important thing.)*

Discovery Questions

1. Arnold differentiates between sin and suffering (pp. 217–218). How are they different? How do they belong together? *(At this point, draw a wheel on a large piece of poster paper. In the hub write "Sin." Ask the group to recall what was shared in response to the open question discussed earlier. Differentiate between those needs caused by sin and those needs which are the suffering that result from sin. For example, "selfish greed" (sin) results in "poverty" (suffering). On each spoke write a specific sin. Where the spoke intersects the rim write the suffering that results. The main point is to help the group see both the difference and connection between sin and suffering.)*

2. What do you think about the saying that if one were to put the evil of the world on one side of a scale and its suffering on the other, the scale would balance (p. 218)? If this were so, how might this affect the way one responds to the need of the world? *(Note the following scripture passages and how they relate to this question: Mt. 4:17, 23–25; 9:35–38.)*

3. Even if the poor are no more spiritually alert than the rich, does this mean we shouldn't try to help them? Why not? *(Note how the above scripture passages also speak to this question.)*

4. What are some of the reasons Arnold cites to reach out to those who are in special need? Can you think of any others?

5. Arnold asserts that the last days have already begun (p. 224). Do you agree? What do you think he means? *(Note: For Arnold, "the last days" do not refer to the period of severe testing as described in the Book of Revelations. Rather, it is more in the sense of Joel's prophecy as in Acts 2:17–21.)*

6. Arnold addresses the tension of becoming too political on the one hand and too complacent on the other. Discuss how this is a tension? Cite examples.

Impact Questions

1. Arnold writes that if we are filled with God's love, we will experience the world's pain ourselves (p. 217). Do you experience such pain? If not, why not? What are some things you could do differently to become more sensitive to the suffering of others?

2. Arnold tells about how his parents didn't worry about exposing him and his brothers and sisters to needy people (as long as there was no sexual impurity). How might this witness speak to your situation?

3. Arnold says that "to be complacent in the face of injustice is a terrible sin" (p. 223). What injustices or evils – especially those closest to you – have you failed to confront or speak out against? What is one thing you can do to move from silence to protest?

4. Arnold warns against cold-heartedness, especially towards those who seem most hopeless. Is there any way you have become cold hearted? How so?

Leader's Questions

_____

_____

_____

_____

_____

_____

_____

_____

_____

_____

Stretching Each Other

Discuss one way you as a group can raise your voice in protest against a current evil or injustice. How might you do this *together?* On the positive side, reflect on how you could reach out together to meet a particular need in your area. Notice that Arnold's examples are personal in nature. He does not refer to efforts of giving money to people or organizations. In this light, how might you as a group personally get involved with a specific need?

Do not push for a particular plan of action. The group may need time to think and pray about this. Perhaps you should wait until you meet next before deciding something. The important thing is that people *feel moved* to do something. The way of love comes from the heart.

Going Forward

Spend time in intercession together. Pray for specific needs the group is aware of. Pray that "the powerful atmosphere of the spirit of Jesus" would penetrate these different situations.

Notes & Announcements

Mission

Preparing

Mission is at the heart of the Gospel. God is a missionary God. This is why he sent his Son into the world (Jn. 3:16). Unfortunately, in today's church, mission is very misunderstood. Some believe it is their duty to convert others and to do so whatever the means. By contrast, others reduce mission to no more than interreligious dialogue and cooperation. Be aware of your own biases toward mission as you study this chapter (pp. 226–233). Pay special attention to what Arnold says mission is not.

For further recommended reading: *The Authentic Witness*, by Norman C. Kraus (Eerdmans).

Getting Started

Get three or four magnets of varying strength (preferably the same size). Also get some metal shavings. On a table (or on an overhead projector) sprinkle the shavings in the pattern of a ring. Place one of the magnets in the center. Show how the strength of a magnet's power determines whether or not the shavings move. Of course, if the magnet itself moves in a given direction then the closer it gets to one side of the ring the more likely it will draw the shavings to itself.

This is meant to illustrate several different facets of mission. The strength and vitality of the center (the magnetic unity and love of community) witnesses to the power of the Gospel. And the more alive the center is the wider its potential influence. At the same time, when the magnetic center moves in a particular direction, whatever is in its path will be affected. You will want to periodically refer to this illustration throughout your study.

Studying Together

Focus Questions

1. Arnold mentions "apostolic mission" several times. What do you think he means by this? What is the character of apostolic mission? When you think of the Apostle Paul, for example, what kind of mission did he embark on?

2. When we seek to reach out to others with the gospel, what should we guard against?

3. What is our first calling as disciples of Jesus? Why is this important?

Discovery Questions

1. Arnold speaks of two "forms of mission" (p. 231). What are these? How do they relate to one another? Need they be in conflict?

2. In our two-fold mission, what should be our primary concern? What, exactly, is our goal? Is it simply the conversion of individuals? How does Acts 26:18 help us understand the purpose of mission?

3. Arnold writes: "The cross is deeply implanted into the earth. It points to heaven, but its outstretched arms express the hunger and thirst of Jesus for all men" (p. 228). What do you think he is trying to get across in this image? What else does this image suggest to you?

4. What do you think Arnold means by the "sharpness" of the gospel (p. 232)? How is this a part of the "good news?"

5. Why is it important that we "are sent by God" when we do mission?

6. Why is unity among believers so important in the missionary task?

7. How would you contrast Arnold's understanding of mission with many of today's evangelistic emphases?

Impact Questions

1. Arnold is clear that mission should "never be a human undertaking" (p. 233). How have you been guilty of human striving in trying to be a witness for Christ? What happens when the Holy Spirit is absent in our efforts to share the gospel?

2. Arnold shares about an instance where his father, Eberhard, refused to speak about the Bruderhof (p. 226). Why? How does this speak to your heart?

3. The urge to reach out to as many people as possible with the gospel is a very legitimate one. However, Arnold warns that in doing this we risk losing the "salt of our witness" (p. 229). Has this ever happened in your life? In your church?

Leader's Questions

_____

_____

_____

_____

_____

_____

_____

_____

_____

_____

Stretching Each Other

Arnold asks a very penetrating question: "Does the world really recognize through today's church that the Father sent Jesus into the world" (p. 227)? How would you assess your church or your group in light of John 17? How might Jesus' prayer become a greater reality among you? Have the group discuss one concrete way it can better express the unity Jesus prays for.

Going Forward

Arnold begins this chapter expressing the deep longing to reach out to other *seeking people* (p. 226). Spend time praying for those who are seeking something different in their lives. Ask God to give you "the right word at the right time for the right person" (p. 226).

Notes & Announcements

_____

_____

_____

_____

_____

_____

_____

_____

_____

Jesus

Preparing

This is a very deep chapter. In many ways it is the centerpiece of Arnold's book. As you read these pages (pp. 237–253), ask God to reveal to you the very heart of Jesus. Seek Jesus himself. Words about Jesus pale in the light of Jesus' personal revelation. Pray for this manifestation, both for yourself and for the group.

For further recommended reading: *Salt & Light,* by Eberhard Arnold (Plough)

Getting Started

On a large poster board, ask the group to share all the names, metaphors, and titles they can think of that the Bible uses to describe Jesus. Highlight the ones Arnold uses. After making your list, ask the group why they think Jesus is described in so many different ways. What does this show us about him? Why is this significant?

Studying Together

Focus Questions

1. How would you describe the mood of this chapter?

2. What do you learn *about* Jesus in this chapter? His birth? life? ministry? death? resurrection?

3. What does believing in Jesus involve? What kind of heart does Jesus come into? Is having Jesus in the heart enough?

4. What, exactly, did (and does) Jesus accomplish? List all the things Jesus accomplished on the Cross.

Discovery Questions

1. Arnold consistently refers to the importance of having "the whole Christ." What does he mean by this? Why is this significant?

2. How is Jesus' weakness, as well as our own, a gift? Why is such weakness a blessing?

3. Arnold refers to John 15 where he believes Jesus speaks from the depth of his heart (pp. 239–240). Read this passage of scripture together. What does it reveal about the kind of relationship Jesus wants with his disciples?

4. What role do feelings play in discipleship? If it's not much help to grasp Jesus with our brains only (p. 243), and if we can't base our Christianity on feelings (p. 242), then what is the Christian to base his faith on?

5. What does dying with Christ mean?

6. How would you explain Arnold's view of the Bible? Is the Bible sufficient in and of itself to reveal Jesus? Why not?

7. What does Arnold mean when he speaks of the Living Word? Arnold says that "the Word is not rigid" (p. 252). Does this mean Arnold is a relativist, or does he mean something else?

Impact Questions

1. What section or passage in this chapter struck your heart most? Why?

2. Arnold says, "We must pray that the knife may cut deeply into our hearts..." (p. 240). When hard times come your way, do you receive them as one who is being pruned? Are you willing to let Jesus' knife cut deeply in your life?

3. How is your heart full of too many other things besides Jesus? Are you hiding any corners of your heart for yourself?

4. Jesus' life was a journey from Bethlehem to Golgotha. How does your life-journey compare to Jesus'? Are you on the same kind of path? Are you willing to go the way of Jesus?

5. Consider your view of and approach to the Bible. In taking the Scriptures seriously there is the temptation to get entangled in the letter and neglect the Living Word. Is there any way you have done this? How can biblical knowledge become an obstacle to a living knowledge of Jesus?

Leader's Questions

_____

_____

_____

_____

_____

_____

_____

_____

_____

_____

Stretching Each Other

Arnold stresses that "Jesus wants us to love *everything* in him" (p. 244). We all have the tendency to ignore or repress certain aspects of Jesus and his teachings. Have the group respond to the following open question: "The hardest thing about Jesus for me personally is _____." If they are willing and able, have each person explain why they find this part of Jesus difficult. Remind them of Jesus' words: "My yoke is easy and my burden is light" (Mt. 11:28–30).

Going Forward

Take what was just shared and submit it in prayer to Jesus. Remind the group that our unwillingness to let Jesus' knife cut our hearts is often the reason we find certain aspects of his life and teaching hard.

Notes & Announcements

_____

_____

_____

_____

_____

_____

_____

The Cross & Salvation

Preparing

Arnold writes: "To receive Jesus we must become silent before God again and again" (p. 254). At the foot of the cross, one must become silent. As you read these two chapters (pp. 254–268), be sure to spend some time in quiet reflection. The mystery of the universe lies not in the atom, but the cross. Ask God to make this mystery alive in your life.

Before the group gathers for this session, ask them to find (or draw) a picture of someone who communicates with their life that he or she is a true Christian. The picture needs to capture the essence of being a Christian.

For further recommended reading: *The Cross of Christ,* by John R. Stott.

Getting Started

Have the group show their pictures to one another. Ask them to share what it is about their picture that indicates that the person represented is a true follower of Jesus.

This activity is meant to illustrate what Arnold writes in the following: "The true Christian is not recognizable outwardly…" (p. 267). In other words, the outer form – whatever it may be – never guarantees the genuineness of faith. In fact, no form is, in and of itself, able to demonstrate whether or not someone is a Christian. This will be important to emphasize throughout your study of these two chapters.

Studying Together

Focus Questions

1. How important is the cross of Jesus in Arnold's mind? Pinpoint those passages that highlight the significance of the cross.

2. What kinds of things did Jesus accomplish on the cross? What kind of salvation does he bring?

3. Describe the "mystery of the cross." What makes it such a deep mystery?

Discovery Questions

1. There is a deep mystery contained in salvation as well. It is related to the mystery of the cross. What is it? *(God wants all to be saved, yet the way to the Father is a narrow way; All things will be reconciled in Christ, yet those bound by sin will not enter the Kingdom. See the following Scripture passages: Ezek. 18:23; 2 Pet. 3:9 – Mt. 7:13–14; 2 Thess. 1:5–10.)*

2. Arnold writes: "The cross is the center of the universe" (p. 255; See also Rev. 5:6; Col. 1:17). What could this possibly mean? If this is true, what difference should it make in our life? How should we live differently from those who do not have the cross in the center of their hearts? (See 2 Cor. 5:13–21; Phil. 2:3–8; 1 Pet. 2:21–23.)

3. Everything one needs to know about the works of the devil is revealed on the cross. Likewise, everything one needs to know about God's love is also revealed on the cross (p. 254). Read Mt. 26:47–27:56 together. The trial and death of Jesus reveals two spirits. Contrast them with each other.

4. What does Arnold mean when he writes: "If we come before God with only our inner burdens, we do him an injustice" (p. 256)?

5. Many things depend upon our own will. However, what are some things we in our own strength cannot bring about?

6. Arnold reminds us that on the cross, "Christ experienced godforsakeness" (p. 257). If Jesus was a faithful, obedient son to the Father, why did God turn his back on him? (See 2 Cor. 5:21.)

Impact Questions

1. Arnold warns against making God too human; of reducing God to our human standard (p. 255). How have you been tempted to do this? How does our culture today do this?

2. "There is an hour of God for everything," writes Arnold (p. 258). Have there ever been times in your life when you have either missed God's hour or preempted it by not patiently waiting for his time?

3. Arnold reminds us that we "cannot serve Jesus out of fear" (p. 261). This is because of the cross. Has your obedience to Jesus been motivated more out of fear, or from love? How?

4. Although Jesus' way is narrow, Arnold writes that it would be terrible if we were to think that we ourselves had found the narrow way, and as a result had no love for those who go the broad way (pp. 263–264). How have you been guilty of such self-righteousness and cold-heartedness? Do you have a love for "sinners" – even the worst kind – as Jesus did?

5. Arnold writes: "Whenever I fail, I keenly feel the words: 'The Lord turned and looked'" (p. 266). How is it with you? Is Jesus so present in your life that when you fail him you see his sad eyes?

6. Arnold emphasizes that "faith is not made up of written precepts" (p. 267). How have you reduced your faith to a set of do's and don'ts, to a set of forms?

Leader's Questions

_____

_____

_____

_____

_____

_____

_____

_____

_____

Stretching Each Other

Throughout _Discipleship_ Arnold lays great emphasis upon two portions of Scripture: (1) the Beatitudes and the Sermon on the Mount (Mt. 5–7) and, (2) the Parable of the Ten Virgins (Mt. 25:1–13). In the latter, Arnold sees a two-fold call to us: to watch and wait, and to call each other to have oil in our lamps (p. 265). Read Mt. 5–7 together and then read the Parable of the Ten Virgins. Remind the group that the oil of which Jesus speaks is the Holy Spirit. Have different ones share where their life's lamp is running dry and how they are not experiencing the greater righteousness that Jesus wants to bring. Are they saying, "Lord, Lord" but not bearing lasting fruit?

Notes & Announcements

_____

_____

_____

_____

_____

_____

_____

_____

The Kingdom of God

Preparing

Too many people misconstrue the meaning of God's kingdom. For some, it is but a synonym for heaven – an invisible or spiritual sphere where God rules. For others, it is the realm of God's reign that comes at the end of time. Still, for others it is an ethical ideal that can be approximated here and now. As you read this chapter (pp. 269–279), pay careful attention to Arnold's understanding of the kingdom of God.

For further recommended reading: *God's Revolution,* by Eberhard Arnold (Plough).

Getting Started

On four separate 3 x 5 cards, describe four different scenes that a small group of people could act out. The scenes are as follows:

- Noah preparing for the Flood
- A couple preparing for the birth of their first child
- Preparing to entertain, in your home, the president, his wife, and a network television crew
- A nation preparing for a massive foreign invasion

Pick four groups to act these scenes out (as a charade). Be sure that these scenes are kept secret. Let the four groups go somewhere else to plan out how they will act out their scene. Have them all gather together and then let each one perform their charade to the group. Have them act their scene out completely. When they are finished, have the rest of the group guess what it is.

The point of this activity is to show how life changes when one is anticipating something important about to happen. Our lives and priorities often get turned upside down when we expect something significant to occur. This is how it should be with the coming of God's kingdom. If we truly expect the coming of God's future reign here on earth, our lives will show it.

Studying Together

Focus Questions

1. How does Arnold contrast the kingdom of God with the kingdoms of this world? Describe the differences.

2. What kind of king is Jesus? How is he different from other rulers?

3. What are some of Arnold's thoughts and feelings about the Last Judgment? *(See also p. 268.)*

Discovery Questions

1. Arnold argues that Jesus "would rather lose his disciples than build his kingdom on a false foundation" (p. 271). What kind of false foundation is Arnold referring to? In what ways might today's church be building on a false foundation?

2. Arnold believes that if God's light enters and moves the hearts of even just two or three people on earth, it has tremendous effects (p. 274). How might this be? Why is even a little crack of light significant? (See Eph. 5:8–16; Mt. 5:14–16; Rom. 13:11–14.)

3. Arnold refers to what Karl Barth once said about the kingdom of God: that it is something that is completely different and independent from us which we cannot mix with our own selves (p. 275). Does this mean there is nothing we can do to prepare for or hasten on the coming of God?

4. If the kingdom of God is built on an entirely different foundation, what kind of foundation would this be? Think radically!

5. Arnold suggests that when we look at today's world as it is now, we see that judgment is already being carried out (p. 278). What does he mean by this? Can you think of some examples how this is so?

Impact Questions

1. How have you tried to make Jesus king but only after he has given you some "bread"? Is your devotion to him conditioned in any way?

2. Arnold boldly asserts: "He who does not wait for the Lord in *every aspect* of his life does not wait at all" (p. 275). This is quite an assertion. Assessing your life and church honestly, what could people see that indicated that indeed you were preparing, expecting, and anticipating God's kingdom? Is your life a preparation for the coming king?

3. Arnold writes: "We do not know how near or far we are from the [final] kingdom of God in terms of time. But we know we can be very near or very far from it in spirit, and that is the decisive question" (p. 276). Are you near or are you far?

Leader's Questions

_____

_____

_____

_____

_____

_____

_____

_____

_____

_____

Stretching Each Other

Have the group imagine for a moment that God had revealed to them, beyond a shadow of doubt, that in one year's time Christ would come back and establish his kingdom on earth. How would the group live differently so as to show the world that God's kingdom was coming soon?

Then ask the group if it really matters whether or not we know the exact timing of God's Final Hour. If, as Arnold says, "the coming of the kingdom is certain, and it is a kingdom of peace, victory, and justice" (p. 277), then what are some concrete ways to demonstrate this?

Going Forward

Spend time together in prayers of thanksgiving for all that God has revealed and done through your study of *Discipleship*. Ask him to show you as a group what to do or be about next. End your time asking for God's kingdom to come in various situations of need.

Notes & Announcements

_____

_____

_____

_____

_____

_____

_____

_____

Appendix A

Who Are You?

Appendix B

About the Bruderhof

Basis

The basis of our communal life is Christ's teaching in the New Testament, especially his words about brotherly love and love of enemies, mutual service, nonviolence and the refusal to bear arms, sexual purity, and faithfulness in marriage.

Instead of holding assets or property privately, we share everything in common, the way the early Christians did as recorded in the Book of Acts. Each member gives his or her talents, time, and efforts wherever they are needed. Money and possessions are pooled voluntarily, and in turn each member is provided for and cared for.

Lunch and dinner are eaten together, and meetings for fellowship, singing, prayer, or decision making are held several evenings a week.

Vision

Though we come from many cultures, countries, and walks of life, we are all brothers and sisters. We are conscious of our shortcomings as individuals and as a community, yet we are certain that it is possible to live out in deeds Jesus' clear way of love, freedom, and truth – not only on Sundays, but from day to day.

We believe that our planet must be conquered for a new social order, a new unity, a new joy. That is, after all, the core of the message Jesus brings. And we must have faith that his message is valid still today.

Family Life

Though many of our members are single adults, the family is the primary unit of our community. Babies and small children receive daily care in our "Children's House" while their parents are at work; preschool, kindergarten, and elementary grades are educated in our own schools.

From the 9th grade, teens attend public high school and then move on to university, college, or technical / vocational training. Some young adults find work in mission service projects and return with valuable knowledge and experience.

Work

We earn our living by manufacturing and selling Community Playthings (a line of play equipment and furniture for children) and Rifton Equipment for People with Disabilities.

Roots

The roots of the Bruderhof go back to the time of the Radical Reformation of early 16th-century Europe, when thousands of so-called Anabaptists left the institutional church to seek a life of simplicity, brotherhood, and nonviolence. One branch of this dissident movement, known as Hutterites after their leader Jakob Hutter, settled in communal villages or Bruderhofs ("place of brothers") in Moravia.

Recent History

In 1920, Eberhard Arnold, a well-known lecturer and writer, left the security of his Berlin career and moved with his wife and children to Sannerz, a tiny German village, to found a small community based on the practices of the early church.

Despite persecution by the Nazis and the turmoil of World War II, the community survived. Amid increasing difficulties in Germany (and expulsion in 1937), new Bruderhofs were founded in England in the late 1930s. In 1940 a second migration was necessary, this time to Paraguay, the only country willing to accept our multinational group. During the 1950s branch communities were started in the United States and Europe. In 1960–61 the South American communities were closed, and members relocated to Europe and the United States. Today there are three Bruderhofs in New York, one in Connecticut, two in Pennsylvania, and two in southeastern England.

Outreach

At a local level, we are involved in voluntary community service projects and prison ministry. On a broader scale, our contacts with other fellowships and community groups have taken us to many places around the globe, especially in recent years. Mission has always been a vital focus of our activity, though not in the sense of trying to convert people or to recruit new members. The connections we make with others outside our communities – with all men and women who strive for brotherhood, no matter what their creed – are just as important to us. We welcome every person who is seeking something new in his or her life. Come join us for a weekend!

For further information, or to arrange a visit, give us a call. We can give you the number and address of the Bruderhof nearest you.
US: 1-800-521-8011 or 412-329-1100   **UK:** 0800 269 048 or +44(0)1580 88 33 44

Appendix C

Roots & Fruits

Appendix D

Gyges' Ring

According to tradition, Gyges (GI-gees) was a shepherd in the service of the King of Lydia. There was a great storm, and an earthquake made an opening in the earth at the place where he was feeding his flock. Amazed at the sight, he descended into the opening, where, among other marvels, he beheld a hollow brazen horse, having doors, behind which, after stooping and looking in, he saw a dead statue. It appeared to him, as more than human, and having nothing on but a gold ring. This he took from the finger of the dead and reascended.

Now the shepherds met together, according to their custom, in order to send their monthly report about the flocks to the king. Gyges came into their assembly, having the ring on his finger, and as he was sitting among them he inadvertently turned the collet of the ring toward the inside of his hand. Instantly he became invisible to the rest of the company and they began to speak of him as if he were no longer present. He was astonished at this, and again touching the ring he turned the collet outwards and reappeared. He made several such trials of the ring, and always with the same result. Upon his amazing discovery, Gyges contrived to be chosen one of the messengers who were sent to the court; where as soon as he arrived, he seduced the queen, and with her help conspired against the king and slew him, and took his kingdom.

Suppose now that there were two such magic rings, and the upright put one of them on and the wicked the other. No person can be imagined to be of such an iron nature that he would stand fast in the way of righteousness. No person would keep his hands off what was not his own when he could safely take what he liked, or go into houses and lie with anyone at his pleasure, and in all respects be like a god among men. After all, don't we all believe in our hearts that injustice is far more pleasurable than justice? Wouldn't we pity the person who, though possessing the power of becoming invisible, became a mere onlooker instead of a partaker of what was not his? Indeed, he would be a most wretched idiot!

Plato, from
The Republic